Coping with Spain

Para Maria del Carmen –
conquistadora –
and Stuart who couldn't come.

Coping with Spain

Garry Marvin

Basil Blackwell

First published 1990

Basil Blackwell Ltd
108 Cowley Road, Oxford, OX4 1JF, UK

Basil Blackwell, Inc.
3 Cambridge Center
Cambridge, Massachusetts 02142, USA

British Library Cataloguing in Publication Data
A CIP catalogue record for this book is available from the
British Library.

Library of Congress Cataloging in Publication Data
Marvin, Garry.
  Coping with Spain / Garry Marvin.
     p.   cm.
  ISBN 0–631–16014–0
  0–631–16832–X (pbk).
  1. Spain—Description and travel—1981—Guide-books.
  I. Title. DP14.M32 1990
  914.6'0483—dc20 89–29526 CIP

Typeset in 10 on 11½pt Garamond
by Photo·graphics, Honiton, Devon
Printed in Great Britain by Billing & Sons Ltd, Worcester

Contents

Acknowledgements

Staff at the Spanish National Tourist Office in London, the Ministry of Tourism in Madrid and many regional tourist offices throughout Spain have been most helpful in supplying information whenever it was required. I would also like to acknowledge the assistance of Ana Badía at RENFE in Madrid, Dr Santiago Guillen, Jan Colbridge and Pat Cronin for trying out an early draft of the manuscript in Spain, and Phil Grabsky who, with his interest in Spanish shadings, offered invaluable comments and information. Special thanks go to Sean Magee, who gave me the opportunity to write this book and who allowed me to develop my interest in the popular art of tourist postal communications; to the reader at Basil Blackwell for his detailed criticism and suggestions; to Mark Allin for his interest and advice at all stages; to Fiona Sewell, for her careful corrections and suggestions; and to Mari Carmen Dominguez Cobos, who for several months had to cope with my questions.

All cartoons are reproduced by kind permission of *Punch*.

Introduction

During the course of most years there are more foreign visitors to Spain than there are native inhabitants (the 1986 census records a national population of just under 38½ million, and in 1987 just over 47¼ million foreigners entered the country). Despite this Spain is a little known country, for the majority of the millions who go there are seeking a relaxing and fun-filled couple of weeks in the sun and head for the coastal resorts, which ably cater for this sort of tourism. The more inquisitive and demanding visitor should not be put off by this image, for it is only necessary to travel a few kilometres inland from the coasts to discover a world of rich cultural and social diversity. Social commentators writing about mass 'package holiday' tourism have often made the point that it provides no promise, or threat, of engagement with the local culture; everything is organized for the visitors and problems are taken care of; the aim is simply to offer the opportunity to 'get away from it all' rather than get involved with another culture or way of life. The aim of this book is to provide assistance for those who do seek to become involved in dealing directly with Spaniards and determining their own exploration of their country.

In a sense, though, the title of this book is a misnomer or at least gives a slightly wrong impression in terms of the idea of 'coping'. During my conversations with people in Spain while collecting material for this book I attempted to explain what sort of book it was to be and what title it was to be given. At this point I ran into a slight difficulty, for I could find no satisfactory translation of the notion of 'coping with Spain'. One possible translation was too strong, for it suggested that the enterprise was a confrontation, while others were neutral, simply suggesting that things have to be arranged. I thought back over my ten pleasurable years of working in and visiting Spain and I realized that indeed one did not have to 'cope' with Spain in any negative sense. It is true that there is a certain knack to getting things done (and I hope it is suitably dealt with in this book) but essentially being in Spain and with Spaniards is simply a pleasure; I am sure that other visitors will find this to be true.

Modern Spain

So what is the Spain you are going to encounter? If I were looking for some general defining quality of the mood of modern Spain it would have to be that of an intense questioning and a powerful sense of change and development – Spain is very much a society on the move, although exactly where and how it is going is what is being questioned. It is impossible to give here more than the briefest of thumbnail sketches of certain elements of this.

Political background

After the civil war of 1936–9 General Francisco Franco and the Nationalist forces emerged triumphant, and Franco remained as head of state until his death in 1975. An understanding of the spirit of modern Spain must be set in the context of the rapid transition since 1975 from the Franco period and all the values he stood for – nationalism, a unified and centralized state, isolation from pernicious foreign influence, Roman Catholic moral and social values and a central focus on the family. At the death of Franco Spanish society emerged from almost four decades of intense social control. Although it is true that the dictator did not have it all his own way at the end of his life and there were processes of social, economic and political change clearly evident, it was impossible under his rule for Spaniards to speak out with complete freedom and voice their opinions about the state of their nation and its society, political system or culture.

After the death of Franco Spain had to go through traumatic and radical political changes, a period referred to as the 'transition', in order to establish a democratic society. Although political changes were occurring during the last years of the dictator, with his death came a crisis; after so many years of dictatorship there was very little of a democratic tradition on which to build. The result of the first years of transition was the 1978 Constitution. This defined the Spanish political and governmental system as a 'parliamentary monarchy', in which the king, Juan Carlos I, as titular head of state has certain constitutional powers, but in which sovereignty resides in the people and is organized through parliamentary democracy. The transition to parliamentary democracy and the legalization of political parties was a difficult time as groups which had enjoyed enormous political and social influence, especially the armed forces and the Catholic church, had to relinquish control. Now firmly established in a democratic mould and with a rapidly changing society, Spain has to live with all the issues which these things raise.

In conversation with Spaniards about political issues you will find that there are several major topics of concern. Perhaps the main area of debate focuses on what the ruling socialist party, the PSOE (Partido Socialista Obero Español – Spanish Socialist Worker Party), under its leader and prime minister Felipe Gonzalez, is really achieving and on concern about the all-embracing power and influence of the party. Now that it has taken power and is firmly established, now that it has in the main dismantled the Franco legacy, the question is what it is actually doing for the country.

Political parties can no longer look backwards to define themselves against the dictatorship. Gone are the days of the reaction to the Franco legacy; people are looking forwards. Although the establishing of democratic institutions and political processes was of central concern during the years of transition this has been, in the main, secured and now parties must concentrate on social and economic issues and what they can offer to the people. Democracy is taken for granted; the concern is with the nature of power and influence exercised by the PSOE and how the administration actually functions at both the national and local level. One only has to look at the enormously critical cartoons (a healthy sign of political freedom) lambasting important political figures in the current affairs magazines to realize that Spaniards are neither fearful nor particularly respectful of these people, and feel that they can be scathing about them in their failures.

The major concerns now are employment (or rather unemployment), education, social and welfare provisions, Spain's relationship with the EEC now that they are full members, their relationship with NATO (there is a strong movement to rid Spain of American military bases) and questions of regional autonomy and what that actually means.

Regional autonomy   The last issue is vast and complex, for it centres on the devolution of certain powers to seventeen autonomous regions. Certain of these, for example Galicia, the Basque country and Catalonia, are well known outside of Spain, but the others are equally zealous in emphasizing and to a certain extent reconstructing their particular socio-cultural identities. The notion of 'reconstruction' is of great importance here because, as a result of Franco's drive to ensure a united Spanish nation (which actually meant 'Castilianization'), the expression of separateness in anything other than the most bland folkloristic manner was prohibited under the dictatorship. The use of any of Spain's languages apart from Castilian (often referred to as Spanish) was forbidden and their public use often prosecuted; and this in a nation where for many Catalan, Basque or Galician was a 'natural' first language and Castilian the second, albeit necessary because public, language. Since 1975 there has been a renaissance of regional cultures, especially in those areas where the culture can be carried by a separate language.

The issues are enormously complex and many would say that the term 'regional' is incorrect. You will find many Basques, Catalans and Galicians who will claim that they are just that – Basques, Catalans and Galicians – first, and only Spanish because they live in the territory of that particular nation state. If you travel in these areas you will see road signs in these languages, public buildings will be flying regional flags, people will speak in a language which you will not immediately recognize and shops, offices, restaurants and bars will have written information in these languages.

Just as these languages to an extent define and unite people, so they can be used to separate them from those who speak Castilian, and some Spaniards complain that when they go to the Basque country or Catalonia they feel unpleasantly isolated in places such as bars where the locals are reluctant to speak to them in Castilian. In the same way as an English-speaking Spaniard might have an easier time of it than an English person in a Welsh-speaking pub, so foreign visitors will have no difficulty in communicating in Castilian, for they are not part of the political problem. If you meet a Basque, Catalan or Galician with whom you can talk about regional or national identities in Spain you are certain to hear some most interesting comments about how *they* have to cope with Spain.

Apart from the social changes brought about by the political condition, perhaps the most significant socio-economic change which has shaped modern Spain has been the movement of population from the countryside to the cities. This movement began during the latter part of the Franco years and has accelerated since then. The essentially rural image of Spain which many still hold must be set beside the fact that the majority of the population now lives in cities. In the last thirty years or so half of the provinces of Spain have suffered a loss of population. Now nine provinces account for about 50 per cent of the population, and the provinces containing Barcelona and Madrid have 25 per cent of the total Spanish population. Within the provinces themselves there has been a drift to the cities.

This population shift naturally reflects a major change in the orientation of the Spanish economy and hence society for, whereas in the 1920s over 50 per cent of the workforce found employment in agriculture, by the 1980s this was reduced to a mere

The cities

18 per cent. Although agriculture is still enormously important in terms of the Spanish economy, new methods, new crops and the need to supply a complex national and international market efficiently have meant a decline in agricultural employment. What these cold statistics represent in terms of people's lives is that ways of life associated with a rural world are changing, people in the cities are acquiring new urban habits and lifestyles and elements of these are filtering back to the rural towns and villages. There are, of course, still thousands of rural communities which, in their differences from modern city life, are fascinating to explore and experience. Life there should not be regarded as a folkloric remnant or picturesque for it is, of course, 'real' life for the inhabitants, but such communities no longer represent Spain; rural life is no longer the mainstream of Spanish life. For that you must look to the vigorous cities with their high-rise blocks housing powerful commercial institutions and the new factories which are creating Spanish wealth.

Although one cannot of course say that Spain is a 'new' country I personally have a sense of Spaniards discovering new potentials; there *is* a new Spain, with its roots in a rich and varied culture, which is vigorous and enormously exciting. Visiting it and exploring it cannot fail to be a stimulating experience.

Preparations

British nationals may enter Spain using either a full
passport or a British Visitor's Passport (so long as
the purpose of travel is either holiday or an unpaid
business trip) without a visa, so long as the stay is
no more than ninety days. If visitors of any
nationality wish to stay for more than ninety days
this can be arranged once you are in Spain. A week
or so prior to the end of that period you must go
to a police station to register the fact that you wish
to stay longer, and they will complete the necessary
formalities. Nationals of other EEC countries, with
the exception of Denmark and Eire whose nationals
do need a passport, may enter using their national
identity cards. Those holding passports from the
United States of America do not need a visa but they
must be in possession of a return ticket. Canadian
nationals do not need a visa, nor do they need to be
in possession of a return ticket. Those who hold an
Australian or New Zealand passport need both a visa
and a return ticket for visits of more than thirty
days, but citizens of these two countries can obtain
an entry permit for up to thirty days at any Spanish
frontier post or at a Spanish airport on production
of their passports.

Just in case of loss or theft of your passport it is
always useful to carry a set of passport-sized
photographs and a photocopy of your birth certificate
with you; this makes the process of being issued a
temporary passport somewhat easier. It is also
advisable to make a note of your passport number
and carry it separately.

Spanish nationals must always carry their identity
cards and foreigners must officially carry adequate
personal documentation (identity card or passport)
with them at all times. In the unlikely event of being

Documents

stopped by the police you will be expected to produce this.

Insurance It is always wise to carry adequate medical, personal and travel insurance when on holiday abroad and you should ask your travel agent for advice. Information about medical insurance is given in the 'Medical matters' chapter and how to go about filling in a police report of theft or loss of personal belongings is covered under 'Emergencies'.

Health The Spanish National Tourist Office advises that there is no risk of diseases such as yellow fever, cholera, typhoid/polio or malaria and there is no reason to take precautions against them. What many visitors are concerned with is the quality of the water and the sensible advice can only be that, although mains water is normally cholorinated, if you are at all worried then drink bottled mineral water (*agua mineral*), which can be bought in litre bottles at bars, grocery shops or supermarkets. If you do think that you might suffer from an upset stomach because of the change in food and water then it is best to buy something from your chemist before you leave home; it will save you the effort of having to cope with a Spanish pharmacy.

Electricity Spanish electricity is usually 220 volts AC (although just occasionally you will come across 115 volts, sometimes in the same room where there is a 220 socket) and sockets take round two-pin plugs. It is therefore advisable to buy one of the small electric-appliance plug adaptors, which deal with most sockets.

Guide books Given the nature of this book it is impossible to give detailed information about Spanish history and culture, so if yours is not to be a lazy beach holiday it is best to carry one of the major cultural guides with you. Which you choose is obviously a matter of taste, but there are four easily available general guides which are well worth considering.

Spain (Phaidon Cultural Guide Series). This is a hardback guide to important examples of Spanish architecture and art organized on a town-by-town basis. It is lavishly illustrated with coloured photographs (and therefore quite expensive) but because of the quantity of pictures there is less detailed information than in the next two books mentioned below. Apart from the photographs there are also ground plans of some of the important buildings and sites, and in the centre there is a set of maps of Spain.

Spain (Michelin Green Guide). Although this has far fewer pages than the Phaidon Guide, the paperback Michelin Guide is perhaps better value if it is wider information you are after. The book starts with a useful set of chapters on geography, economy, history and art/architecture, and the main section dealing with important sights in each town and city contains a wealth of detailed information. Although there are no colour illustrations there are line drawings, but what are particularly useful for walking to places of interest are the maps of town centres. This is a highly recommended guide.

Spain: The Mainland (Ernest Benn Blue Guide Series). Prefaced with chapters on history, architecture and painting this guide gives excellent information about the sights of cultural interest, and for each town there is a short historical outline. For those who are on a driving tour of Spain this is a particularly valuable guide because, apart from the detailed set pieces on the towns and cities, it is organized according to various routes between cities, giving information about the smaller towns and villages you pass en route. If there is someone in the car who can read as well as navigate while you are driving, this can therefore make a journey across country much more interesting, even if it is only by noting that one of the *conquistadores* was born in the tiny Extremaduran village which you are driving past. Because it gives so many snippets of fascinating information about even the smallest places you may well be tempted to explore places which you did not expect would detain you.

Spain (Insight Guides Series – APA Publications). This book is rich in evocative coloured photographs and gives good, general, cultural information in a region-by-region format. It is particularly good for quite detailed (for a guide book) essays on Spanish history, politics, society and art – the combination of these gives an excellent introduction to Spain and a background against which to understand and appreciate what you see.

Phrase book   Although this book contains words and phrases which you might find useful for coping with various situations it is really advisable to have a more comprehensive book with you. There are several on the market but perhaps the very best is the Berlitz *Spanish for Travellers*, which has sections on arrival in the country, accommodation, eating out (with a particularly good list of items which might be encountered on menus), travelling, sightseeing, making friends, changing money and medical matters as well as a very useful general reference section. Also included is a 25-page dictionary which should cover most of your requirements, although should you really wish to develop your Spanish vocabulary then take a look at the pocket-sized *Collins Spanish Dictionary*.

Free information   Tourism is an enormously important industry in Spain and the government has recently encouraged the development of interest in more than the package-tour coast; it is attempting to promote that which has been seriously neglected by the majority of summer visitors – Spanish culture. The result is that regional tourist offices are producing high-quality booklets (many of them quite substantial) and information packs which cover everything from accommodation, cuisine and wine to local historical guides and information about museums, festivals, handicrafts and excursions from particular centres. If you know which parts of Spain you will be visiting a wealth of information can be obtained simply by writing to your country's Spanish National Tourist Office (addresses below), telling them where you intend to go and asking for information about that region. Do *write* to them, though – it is almost impossible to get through on the telephone; and send a large stamped addressed envelope. (Please note that the National Tourist Office cannot make bookings for you.)

Once you have the information from them you will find in the booklets lists of addresses of regional and local tourist offices in Spain. It is worth writing to these (this can be done in English) as they will be able to send you an even greater range of information.

Spanish National Tourist Office
57 St James Street
London SW1A 1LD
UK
Tel: 01-499 0901

Spanish National Tourist Office
665 Fifth Avenue
New York
New York 10022
USA
Tel: 212-759 8822

National Tourist Office of Spain
Water Tower Place, Suite 915
East 845, North Michigan Avenue
Chicago Ill 60611
USA
Tel: 312-944 02 15

National Tourist Office of Spain
5085 Westheimer
The Gallery Building Suite 4800
Houston, Tex 77056
USA
Tel: 713-840 7411

National Tourist Office of Spain
8383 Wiltshire Blvd, Suite 960
Beverly Hills, Cal 90211

Useful addresses and telephone numbers

USA
Tel: 213-658 71 88/89

Spanish National Tourist Office
60 Bloor Street West
201 Toronto
Ontario M4V 3B8
Canada
Tel: 416-961 3131

Spanish National Tourist Office
International House, Suite 44
104 Bathhurst Street
PO Box A-9675
Sydney
New South Wales
Australia
Tel: 02-264 7966

Climate

Despite Spain's image of being a country of sun it has a far from uniform climate. As a general rule it can be said that if you visit Spain during the late spring or summer you are unlikely to have to suffer rain, which in most parts of Spain falls in early spring, autumn and winter. However, you must remember that Spain is a peninsula having over 8000 km of coastline, with some 900 km dividing the northern Atlantic coast from the southernmost part near the Mediterranean, and with a high, mountainous interior, so it is worth giving a general outline of the main climatic divisions of the country. The Spanish National Meteorological Institute divides the country into three distinct zones – the Atlantic or Green Zone, the Continental Zone and the Mediterranean Zone. The Balearics are usually included in the last of these but the Canaries, because of their almost tropical climate, are usually regarded as separate from the main peninsular zones.

Atlantic/ Green Zone

The first important sub-area here is Galicia, which is itself divided between the coastal and valley area and the mountainous interior. In summer the average coastal temperatures range from approximately 24 °C (75 °F) to 26 °C (79 °F), so even being on the most northerly beaches is usually pleasant. Both spring and autumn temperatures are mild but there is high rainfall. In the interior the temperatures are generally mild in the spring and summer and cold with considerable rainfall in the winter.

The other sub-area is the Cantabrian Corniche – the coastal zone running from Asturias through the Basque country to Navarre – which is generally more cloudy and therefore has less guaranteed sunshine in the summer, but where the temperatures are pleasantly warm. In Santander, for example, temperatures range from approximately 19 °C (67 °F) to 22 °C (72 °F). Winter is a particularly rainy season on the coast, and inland it is cold with frequent snowfalls.

Continental Zone

The northern plateau area, roughly extending from Valladolid to Soria, is generally hot in summer, but the nights can be cool. Spring and autumn are relatively short with warm, pleasant temperatures but winters are cold and the temperature can drop to as low as 2 °C (36 °F).

The southern plateau has a similar climate but summers are noticeably hotter and drier, in Madrid for example ranging from 26 °C (79 °F) to 31 °C (88 °F), and the winters can be bitterly cold – again, Madrid's temperature ranges between 5 °C (41 °F) and 9 °C (48 °F) although it can fall even lower. Most of the rainfall occurs in the autumn but spring can also be rainy.

The River Ebro basin area has hot, dry summers and cold, dry winters, although this very much varies with altitude. For example, Zaragoza, the main city in this zone, has summer and winter temperatures very similar to those of Madrid. Spring and autumn are both mild with most of the rainfall occurring in these seasons. A particular climatic feature in this region is the strong northwesterly/westerly wind known as *el bierzo*.

In the west of the Continental Zone is the Extremaduran region which has extremely hot summers, in Cáceres for example between 29 °C (84 °F) and 33 °C (91 °F), and cold winters – 7 °C (45 °F) to 12 °C (54 °F). Snow is rare and most precipitation occurs as rain in the early spring and autumn.

The basin of the Guadalquivir River in southwest Andalusia forms the last region within this zone. Summers are extremely hot and some of Spain's highest temperatures are recorded here. The summer temperature in Seville ranges between 32 °C (90 °F) and 36 °C (97 °F), although it can often pass 40 °C (104 °F) to reach a leaden 47 °C (117 °F). In a hollow on the road from Seville to Cordoba is the town of Ecija, which becomes so hot in the summer that it

is known as *el sarten de Andalucía* (the frying pan
of Andalusia). Spring and autumn are generally warm
seasons with only moderate rainfall. Most rain falls
in the winter and very early spring.

The general description of this climatic zone found
in school geography texts is that of hot, dry summers
and mild, wet winters. In the Catalonian part of
the zone for example Barcelona normally registers
summer temperatures between approximately 19 °C
(66 °F) and 25 °C (77 °F) and winter temperatures
between 6 °C (43 °F) and 13 °C (56 °F). Spring
and autumn are long, temperate seasons with only
modest rainfall although this area sometimes suffers
short, localized, torrential downpours in the
autumn.

**Mediterranean
Zone**

Further south, the Valencian and Murcian part of
the zone has somewhat hotter summers with a very
high annual average of hours of sunshine. In Valencia
itself summer temperatures can range between 23 °C
(74 °F) and 29 °C (84 °F). As with the Catalonian
region the winter is very short and mild.

Finally the southernmost part of the zone, the
Mediterranean and Atlantic coast region of Andalusia,
has very hot summers with temperatures in Almeria
between 22 °C (72 °F) and 30 °C (86 °F), and San
Fernando, just south of Cadiz, has the highest annual
average hours of sunshine of the entire peninsula.
Spring and autumn are pleasantly warm with very
little rainfall – in fact the province of Almeria has
the lowest rainfall of Spain – and the winters,
especially in the eastern areas, are renowned for
their warmth. Along parts of the Atlantic coast of
Cadiz there is an unpleasant wind known as the
Levante which can sometimes blow for several
days at a time. It is, in part, this unpredictable
wind, strong enough just to lift the sand on the
beach and make sitting there disagreeable, which
has kept this coastline less developed touristically
than that of the Mediterranean.

The Balearics are included in the Mediterranean
zone but here the sea winds moderate the more
suffocating effects of the summer heat. The highest

rainfall is recorded on the islands between September and December.

The Canaries   These islands, because of their southern latitude, have a very special and thoroughly agreeable climate all year round. Throughout the year the temperatures are remarkably stable between approximately 20 °C (68 °F) and 27 °C (81 °F). There is very little rainfall and that mainly on the easternmost islands. Izaña, situated in the inner highlands of Tenerife, registers the highest annual average hours of sunshine of all Spain – 3397 hours.

Getting there

The main choice you have to make with regard to air travel to Spain from Britain is whether to travel by scheduled flights or by charter flights. There are an enormous number of cheap charter flights into Spain, especially during the spring and summer seasons, and it is worth spending time checking for cheap deals with travel agents and in the travel pages of newspapers and magazines such as London's *Time Out*. It is also worth ringing the Air Travel Advisory Bureau (01-636 5000), a free service, which will give you details of the cheapest flights in various travel agents and bucket shops in London. It is possible to find some incredibly cheap flights to airports which serve the main holiday areas (remember to ask whether the prices quoted include airport taxes). It is also worth noting that with most charter flights you will be restricted to a stay defined in units of seven days, so for example seven, fourteen or twenty-one days.

Of the British and Spanish flag carriers, British Airways offers direct daily flights from London Heathrow to Madrid and Barcelona, daily from Gatwick to Malaga and daily, with the exception of Saturday, from Gatwick to Bilbao. Iberia, the national airline of Spain, offers flights (most of them daily) from Heathrow to thirteen airports in Spain (Alicante, Barcelona, Bilbao, Ibiza, Las Palmas, Madrid, Mahon [Menorca], Malaga, Palma de Mallorca [the importance of tourism is attested by the fact that this airport handles more international passengers than any other in Spain], Santiago, Seville, Tenerife and Valencia). It also has flights from Luton to Mahon and Malaga, from Gatwick to Madrid and from Manchester to Barcelona, Madrid, Malaga and Palma. Some of these flights may in fact be with Aviaco, the other national

By air

"Only a small point, but the Aviation Authority prefer we call it rest period rather than siesta."

airline, but booking is through Iberia. Iberia often offers special price tickets, such as its Money Saver fare (which actually allows you to fly into one city and out from another), and it is certainly worth checking the price of the scheduled flights, which often work out to be not much more than many charter tickets. The advantage of such tickets is that there are no hidden extras, the flights are at convenient times and for a flexible duration, and you can also make use of special offers such as their Fly and Drive car-hire scheme, which works out much cheaper than hiring a car once in Spain.

From the United States Iberia offers a daily direct flight to Madrid from New York and on certain days of the week from Miami, Chicago and Los Angeles. Pan American, TWA and American Airlines also have regular flights to Madrid. Air Canada has a flight on four days of the week from Toronto to Madrid via Lisbon. Qantas have no flights from Australia to Spain and advise that the best way is to fly via London. Similarly Air New Zealand only fly to London and Frankfurt in Europe, and flights with them are best routed through one of these two cities.

From airport to city

All the international airports mentioned above have very cheap, regular bus or coach services to and from the centre of the cities, so you should not have to pay for a taxi unless you particularly want to. Barcelona has a direct train service during the day from the airport (the station can be reached from within the terminal itself), which will take you to the main station, Barcelona-Sants, which is the last stop. Malaga airport is also served by a rail link which goes to Malaga's main station.

Duty-free shops

You will find duty-free shops in the airports of Madrid, Barcelona, Malaga, Alicante, Palma de Mallorca and Valencia. There are also duty-free shops at Seville, Gerona, Ibiza and Mahon, but these are only open during the main tourist season and if you are leaving from one of these aiports out of season it is best to buy your wines and spirits in a local supermarket, where the wines are likely to be only slightly more expensive than duty-free and where you will probably find a greater range. Sometimes airline duty-free prices may be cheaper so it is worth checking the airline price list on the outward flight and making a comparison. The risk is that the stocks are limited on the planes and they might not have what you want.

By ship

Brittany Ferries offer the only direct car and passenger service from England to Spain. They sail twice a week from Plymouth to Santander and the crossing takes 24 hours. It is not a particularly cheap way to travel because you will have to pay for the car and passengers and on top of that for accommodation aboard. This accommodation ranges from four-berth cabins with no facilities to extremely comfortable two-berth cabins with shower/WC. Children under four pay about half the adult fare, which is a good deal cheaper than the full-price airfare they would incur. On board food is not particularly cheap and in the high season you can expect long waits standing to get it.

The great advantage of this crossing is that you do have your car with you, which gives you great freedom. There are no luggage restrictions, which means that you can bring back even more wine, olive oil and ropes of garlic, or even larger straw donkeys from Mijas.

If you have decided to travel with your own car then sailing to Santander will obviously save you an enormous number of kilometres compared with crossing the Channel and driving through France. Brittany Ferries calculate that difference between the return trip Santander–Marbella and Calais–Marbella as 2404 km, and although their suggested route through France and Spain is not exactly direct (in order to make use of motorways) it is of course true that it is much more tiring to drive through France than to sit on a ship, and you do save on petrol and accommodation. (The ship is not quite so pleasant, though, if you are trying to settle yourself through one of the famous Bay of Biscay storms – Richard Ford, a nineteenth-century traveller in Spain, described it as the 'sleepless Bay of Biscay'. Don't forget this is not a Channel crossing; you will be on the ship for 24 hours.)

Frontier and customs posts

If you are driving into Spain from France, Portugal or Gibraltar – and there are some thirty-six points for entering Spain – then it is worth noting the opening times of customs posts. The main points of entry such as the Irún–Hendaye (on the Irún Motorway between France and the Guipuzcoa Basque province), those at Port-Bou–Cerbere, la Junquera–Le Perthus and Puiggerda–Bourg Madame (between France and the Catalan province of Gerona) and those between Seo de Urgel and Andorra are open permanently, but some of the smaller posts are only open from early morning until late in the evening, and the actual times vary according to the season. The customs posts between Spain and Portugal are either open permanently during the spring and summer seasons or are open between about 08.00 and 13.00 at other times, with a few remaining open until 22.00. The Gibraltar border is open permanently for those with nothing to declare, but for those with goods to declare the customs post is open between 08.00 and 21.00 daily. You can expect delays of up to an hour in the summer at the Gibraltar crossing and the customs will often check your car for items such as televisions and other electrical domestic goods.

A complete list of customs posts and their times of opening is available from the Spanish National Tourist office.

By train

If you are travelling from Britain to Spain by train you will have to go via Paris and change there. From Paris Austerlitz there is a direct overnight service (with couchette accommodation) to Madrid, so it is possible to leave London early in the morning and arrive in Madrid early the following morning. Return tickets are usually valid for one month and can be booked either through a travel agent or at a British Rail ticket office.

By coach

This can be a particularly cheap way of travelling to Spain, although it is worth comparing the price against the available charter offers. The coaches, however, all go through France and you will be stuck on the coach for the best part of two days if you are going to the far south (although the London–Barcelona coaches do the run in 24 hours), so don't expect to arrive particularly refreshed. An advantage of coach travel is that departure and return dates are more flexible than charter flights and you can get open returns. As with charter flights, advertisements appear in newspapers and magazines such as *Time Out*, or you can contact the Coach Travel Centre in London (see below). It is also worth checking with your local travel agents and coach companies who may well offer such trips.

British Airways
75 Regent Street
London W1R 1FJ
Tel: 01-897 4000 (call queuing system operates)

Iberia Airlines of Spain
130 Regent Street
London W1
Tel: 01-437 9822

Note: it is often impossible to get through on the London number and quicker to use the Aberdeen (0224-591453) or Glasgow (041-248 6581) numbers.

Iberia Airlines of Spain
Toll-Free Number in USA 800-221-9714

Air Travel Advisory Board
Tel: 01-636 5000

Brittany Ferries
Millbay Docks
Plymouth PL1 3EW
Tel: 0752-221321

The Coach Travel Centre
13 Regent Street
London SW1
Tel: 01-730 0202

Internal travel

Spain is particularly well served by its domestic network. Iberia and Aviaco operate regular national flights to thirteen peninsular airports (Madrid, Santiago, Oviedo, Bilbao, Vitoria, Barcelona, Valencia, Alicante, Almeria, Granada, Malaga, Seville and Jerez), to three airports in the Balearics (Ibiza, Palma and Mahon), to six in the Canaries (Arrecife, Puerto del Rosario, Las Palmas, Santa Cruz de Tenerife, Santa Maria de Valverde and Santa Cruz de La Palma) and to Melilla, the Spanish territory on the North African coast. Although many of these flights do originate in Madrid there are also very good daily connections (often with several flights a day) between many of the major cities. If you have to travel long distances, when speed and comfort might be worth paying extra for, it is worth checking the price of air tickets; these are often quite reasonable and on some days and some routes (especially at night) there are discount fares available. Information about fares and routes can be obtained from Iberia offices and most travel agencies.

RENFE, the national railway company, proudly announces that there are some 13,500 km of track, that 2500 cities, towns and villages have stations and that since the reforms of the late 1970s rail travel has improved immensely. The problem with rail travel, as a quick glance at a map will show you, is that it is essentially a radial system centred on Madrid with few good links between other major cities, so to get about the country without going through Madrid sometimes requires tortuous routings. But rail travel is comparatively cheap and the trains on the major intercity routes are generally comfortable. The flagships of the system are the TALGO trains, which operate on the major distance routes. They offer airconditioning, reclining seats, videos, snack bars and/or restaurant cars and have preferential treatment on the tracks, so their travel time is shorter than that of other trains on the same route.

There is a bewildering array of types of train and the price of your ticket will, in part, depend on the sort of train you get. Apart from the TALGO there are Expresos and Rápidos (which are not actually that *rápido*), Electrotrenes, TER, Automotores and Tranvías. You should not worry about these differences and perhaps the only important consideration for the tourist is whether it is worth paying the extra money for the faster and more comfortable TALGO on long-distance trips.

On many of the long-distance overnight trips there is sleeping accommodation available. There are two types of such accommodation on Spanish trains: the luxurious *coche camas* (sleeping car) of the International Wagon Lits company, which consists of individual compartments and which is expensive (for example, it is cheaper to fly from Seville to Madrid than to travel in the *coche camas*); and the cheaper *literas* (couchettes), which are quite comfortable and have sheets, blankets and pillows provided – though these are somewhat cramped, with six bunks per compartment. It is probably best to try to book the top bunks because you can command the extra luggage space at the head of the bunk. If you do take a trip in a *litera* on a long journey during the summer you would be well advised to take a bottle of mineral water with you, because it does get hot. The water is also useful for brushing your teeth in the morning but it is best to have uncarbonated water; it can be difficult rinsing out toothpaste with fizzy water.

Some trains have snack bars and/or restaurants (and stewards will also come through the carriages with a refreshment cart), but both are quite expensive and the food in the snack bars is not particularly good; so it is probably best to provision yourself with a couple of hefty *bocadillos* (filled rolls), which can be bought at the bars which are inevitably found in or near the station. Quite often you will find that when the train stops at a major station there will be people selling drinks and snacks on the platform alongside the train, and you will have time to get off and buy from them.

Some 132 railway stations (*estaciones de trenes*) have advanced booking facilities and 81 of these are computer linked. There are also hundreds of travel agents (*agencias de viajes*) throughout Spain, which are able to make bookings and sell rail tickets through their computer links with the central reservation office. You are likely to want either a single ticket (*un billete de ida*) or a return ticket (*ida y vuelta*) in either first class (*primera clase*) or second class (*segunda clase*). When you make a reservation for a long-distance train it is worth paying the small charge which will allow you to reserve a particular seat. The illustration explains how to read your ticket and find your seat.

Billetes
(tickets)

If you are buying your ticket at a railway station you should look for the signs *largo recorrido* for the ticket window for long-distance journeys and *cercanias* for short journeys.

You can also make reservations for intercity and international journeys without stirring from your hotel room, by calling, or having the reception desk in the hotel call, the central reservations office in Madrid (91 429 82 28), which is open between 09.00 and 21.00 every day of the week. These reservations can be made between one month and two hours prior to the departure of the train. Once a reservation has been made you will be given a five-figure code which identifies your reservation and you must then go to any station or travel agent which sells rail tickets to pay for and obtain the tickets. This must be done within two days of having made the reservations. You may pay for these tickets with cash, Eurocheques, Visa, Mastercard-Eurocard or 4B credit card. Although it is possible to obtain a reimbursement for an unused ticket paid for with cash, this is not possible if you have paid with credit card. It is also possible, prior to the date of travel

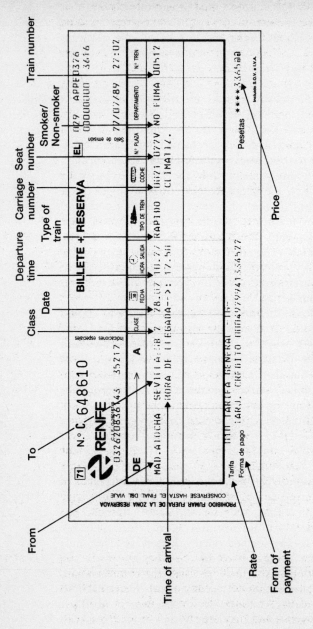

How to read a Spanish Intercity rail ticket

and at the place where you bought the ticket or at any other station or travel agent, to change the date, train or class of ticket.

RENFE offers an enormous variety of reductions on tickets. My particular favourite is the series of discounts available for families. There is, for example, a discount of 20 per cent for what are called 'First Category' families with four children, 40 per cent for 'Second Category' families with seven children and a magnificent 50 per cent discount for a family '*Categoría de Honor*' with ten children. There are, however, discounts which are more likely to be useful for the average traveller or family.

Note   Most of these tickets apply only on blue days (*días azules*) in the RENFE calender. As a general rule Monday to Thursday and Saturday are blue days; Friday and Sunday are white days, when discounts do not apply. This is because of the expected numbers of travellers on those days, particularly those going home or back to work after a week away and young men on weekend leave during military service. There are a few other days in the year, days which normally coincide with special holidays, when the blue day fares do not apply. Details of these dates can be found at railway stations or at travel agents.

The simplest discounts apply to return tickets. On long journeys, what RENFE calls *largo recorrido* – over 200 km – you will be entitled to a 20 per cent discount if you both travel out and return on blue days. There is also a 25 per cent discount on day-return journeys for short trips (with a minimum of 100 km for the total journey). These day-return journeys can be made on any day except Sundays and holidays.

Children   Children under the age of four may travel free on any train (and this includes sleeping accommodation) so long as they do not occupy a seat. Those between four and twelve years old are eligible for a 50 per cent discount and they are entitled to occupy a seat.

Families   RENFE offers a Family Card (*Tarjeta Familiar*) which can be purchased, on the presentation of passports, for a nominal cost at any of the agencies which sell rail tickets. To qualify for this ticket there must be a minimum of three people in the family, but this can be two adults and one child (under the age of twenty-five). The ticket can be used on a journey (on blue days) over 100 km. With a Family Card the first adult pays the full ticket price but any other adult family member receives a 50 per cent discount and children between the ages of four and twelve receive a 75 per cent discount. Once again children under the age of four travel free.

Young people   A Young Person's Card (*Tarjeta Joven*) is available for those between the ages of twelve and twenty-six. This ticket can be obtained from railway ticket offices or travel agents and you will need to show your passport and hand in a passport-sized photograph to obtain it. These cards are valid for travel from 1 May until 31 December (but they may be purchased two months before that date) and are valid for single journeys over 100 km or 200 km return journeys. This card cost just under £15 in 1989 but entitles the holder to a 50 per cent discount on tickets, and the use of a couchette (*litera*) on overnight journeys is free. There is a 'couchette coupon' (*cupón litera*) attached to the card. Do take care of this card, though, because if it is lost or stolen RENFE will not replace it.

InterRail   Those under the age of twenty-six can also make use of the international InterRail card in Spain. In Britain, this card can be purchased at principal British Rail stations and many travel agents and you must show your passport when making the application. The card is valid for one month for unlimited travel in twenty-one countries, but you may have to pay a supplement on certain trains and for sleeping accommodation. Details of these and reservations can be obtained from British Rail travel centres.

It is also worth considering paying the extra and purchasing the InterRail + Boat ticket, which allows discounts or free travel on some Mediterranean, Scandinavian and Irish shipping routes. In terms of

Spain this applies to certain routes between Spain and Morocco operated by Trasmediterranea (see the section on peninsula–island travel below).

If you do not live in Britain and wish to purchase Spanish rail cards prior to arrival in Spain, it is best to ask your local travel agents which cards they can sell you.

Tourist card

A person of any age, resident outside Spain, may apply for a Tourist Card (*Tarjeta Turista*) valid for various periods of unlimited travel on any train. The card can be purchased from RENFE's European office in Paris, from major stations and some travel agents in Britain and from RENFE travel offices and the railway stations of Barcelona, Madrid, Irún, and Port-Bou in Spain. The card is valid for one year from the date of purchase but you must stipulate the date on which you wish the card to commence either at the time of purchase or within six months from the date on which you purchase it. This validation of the card can be carried out at main railway stations or agencies selling RENFE tickets.

Eurail

There is also an international ticket called Eurail, available to those who are resident *outside* Europe, which is valid in Spain. This must be obtained outside of Spain in a travel agency or in the offices of the European rail companies concerned. It is valid for first class travel on any train in Spain (as it is in the other countries which belong to the scheme) and for unlimited distances. You will, however, have to pay the supplements for sleeping cars or couchettes. There is a junior version of this card called Eurail Youth Pass, available for those under twenty-six and valid for second class travel.

Narrow gauge railways

Although RENFE is the main Spanish railway operator there is one other company, called FEVE, which operates a few narrow gauge railways in the Cantabrian area, on Mallorca and between Cartegena and Los Nietos in Murcia. The lines which pass along the Cantabrian Corniche and the immediate hinterland, especially that which links El Ferrol (the birthplace of Franco) with Santander and Bilbao, make for a visually exciting journey for tourists, as do the linked lines which go south to Leon and then west to Bilbao. There are three trains a day in each direction between Ferrol and Gijon, Oviedo and Santander, Santander and Bilbao, and Bilbao and Leon. The Madrid office of FEVE will send you a map of these routes and details of prices; the address can be found at the end of this section.

Train cruises RENFE offers several of what it calls train cruises, a rather interesting way of visiting particular areas. The most substantial of these is the Al Andalus Expreso, which is a luxurious train/hotel. The trips last either four or five days, beginning and ending in Seville and visiting Cordoba, Granada, Malaga and Jerez. Apart from the sleeping cars the train has vintage pullman carriages, with superb period decoration and furnishings, which are used as saloon cars, as well as bars and a restaurant where meals consist of regional cuisine. The train even has a fully-fitted shower car. The price includes accommodation, breakfast and evening meal and all the guided excursions. The high price of the trip reflects the quality of the service offered.

FEVE offers a similar style of excursion on the Transcantábrico, which makes a week-long 1000-km trip between Leon and El Ferrol. The carriages have a more modern design than the Al Andalus but are equally well appointed. Because the Cantábrico is a narrow gauge railway it can take tight curves and steep gradients and thus travel through the often mountainous countryside. The route along the Cantabrian coast and through the mountains of the Picos de Europa is stunning. The train has similar facilities to those of the Al Andalus but meals are taken at traditional inns or restaurants. These trips can be booked in Britain and the United States through the RENFE/FEVE appointed agents (see below). Those from other countries should make applications through their local travel agents.

There are shorter trips from Madrid offered by RENFE, for example a weekend in Salamanca or a

Guadalupe–Trujilo–Cáceres journey, and there are day excursions, with guided tours included in the price, to Aranjuez (on the strangely named 'Strawberry' Train, which is pulled by a steam locomotive), Sigüenza, Cáceres and Cuenca. All of these RENFE trips can be booked through travel agencies or at main RENFE offices in Madrid.

A recent Spanish railways publication should be very helpful if you are thinking of spending some time travelling on long-distance trains. The *Atlas de Ferrocarriles Españoles* (Atlas of Spanish Railways) has a very good set of maps of Spain (which can also be used for driving) showing the train routes. All towns and villages are marked so you can see the rail connections, there are thematic maps of the main routes and maps with the railway distance between towns. Information about local services from major cities is given, as are the telephone numbers of the main stations. There are also very useful city maps and for the largest the surrounding area is also included. This map book will be on sale in bookshops but you can obtain a copy direct from RENFE. You can write in English to:

Timetables and general information

Gabinete de Información y Relaciones Externas
RENFE
Avenida Pio XII s/n
Madrid 28036
Tel: 733-60 37

For those travelling by rail in Europe, Thomas Cook publish a monthly European timetable and a rail map of Europe. These may be purchased at Thomas Cook travel shops or directly from their publishing house (see address below).

Useful addresses and telephone numbers For RENFE representatives outside of Spain:

Europe
1–3 Avenue Marceau
75116 Paris
France
Tel: 47-23 52 00

America
Avenida Corrientes, 311–3º
Buenos Aires
Argentina
Tel: 311-96 57

For RENFE information:

RENFE
Dirección de Información
Madrid–Chamartin
28036 Madrid
Spain
Tel: 733-62 00
Telephone reservations: 91-429 82 28

For FEVE information:

FEVE
General Rodrigo 6–3º
(Parque de las Naciones)
28003 Madrid
Spain
Tel: 91-253 76 56

For RENFE/FEVE train cruises:

Marsans Travel
7a Henrietta Place
London W1M 9AG
Tel: 01-493 4934

Marsans Travel
205 East 42nd Street
Suite 1514
New York 10017
Tel: 212-661 6565

or

Marsans Travel
3325 Wilshire Blvd
Suite 508
Los Angeles
California 90010
Tel: 738-8016

For Thomas Cook timetables:

Thomas Cook Timetable Publishing
(TPO/F)
PO Box 36
Peterborough PE3 6SB
UK

By bus

There are many long-distance buses/coaches (*autobuses* or *autocares* – but in the Canaries buses have the delightful name of *guagua*, which is pronounced almost as 'wa-wa') between major cities and from smaller towns and cities to important provincial centres. It is difficult, however, to give detailed, useful information about them because they do not belong to any national system. Long-distance coaches are much cheaper than trains, are often faster and have better connections. These coaches are often very comfortable and offer reclining seats, airconditioning and videos.

To find out what services are available it is best to ask in the local tourist office, at a travel agent or at the bus station (*estación de autobuses*) itself. It is also worth looking in the yellow pages of the telephone directory under *autocares*, where you will see block adverts for long-distance coaches. The coach company ENTACAR has been increasing its services, so look up its address to check on routes. RENFE also runs certain long-distance buses from major railway stations to places where they do not have good or any train connections.

By hired car

If you do not have your own car with you and yet you want the freedom of travelling when and where you will, then car hire (*alquiler de coches*) is the answer. International companies such as Hertz, Avis and Europcar have extensive networks in peninsular Spain as well as in the Canaries and the Balearics, as do the major national car-hire companies Atesa and Ital, which tend to be cheaper than the internationals. Most airports have several car-hire desks and their offices can also be found in most towns and cities.

If you are hiring from within a city then it is worth checking the prices offered by the smaller local firms, which offer considerably cheaper rates. Once again the local tourist office or a travel agent should have details of companies, but you can also check in the telephone guide yellow pages. At Malaga airport (and sometimes at others where there is a lot of tourist traffic) you will find representatives of local companies approaching people who look as if they want to rent cars. Most of these are perfectly reputable (but do check the documents carefully) and offer very good deals.

There are various rates which are useful for tourists – per day or per week with a kilometre charge, unlimited kilometres on a weekly rate and weekend rates with a certain number of kilometres free. With the international or national companies you will be able to hire in one place and drop off at another, but check to see if there is an extra charge for this.

To hire a car you will have to be over twenty-one years old and hold a current driving licence. It is best to have an international driving licence with you although this will often not be asked for. It is best, but not obligatory, to pay the small extra for personal accident insurance and the collision damage waiver. An IVA tax (equivalent to British VAT) of 12 per cent will be added to the total transaction. The simplest way to hire is to use a credit card, but the bill can always be paid in pesetas when you return the car. Most companies will also change the category of your booking to your advantage when you come to make the payment. So for example, if you have hired for several days on an unlimited kilometre rate, but you have not done many kilometres and it would have been cheaper to have hired at a daily rate and paid for the distance travelled, this will usually be done for you when you return the car.

Outside Spain, you can make hire-car bookings with Spanish companies through their London representatives:

ITAL
Car Hire Centre

23 Swallow Street
London WC1
Tel: 01-734 7661

or

ATESA
7a Henrietta Place
London W1M 9AG
Tel: 01-493 4934

By hitchhiking

Hitchhiking is legal in Spain and, although it is not encouraged, you are unlikely to have problems with the police. It is not, however, an efficient way of travelling, for Spaniards are not particularly keen to give lifts and if you do get a lift it is unlikely to be a long one. If you are attempting to hitch you can slightly improve your chances of being picked up if you are reasonably smartly dressed. If you are planning to hitchhike in Spain you can apply for the International Hitchhiking Card (*Carnet de Auto-Stop*). This provides you with an insurance policy giving unlimited cover for costs and injuries resulting from any accident. This card can be obtained from:

Delegación Española de la Federación Internacional de Camping
(Servicio Auto-Stop)
Edificio España (Grupo 4º Piso 11, Oficina 4)
Madrid 28013
Spain
Tel: 91-242 10 89

By lift-sharing

An alternative to hitchhiking is lift-sharing – a system by which you share the petrol costs with a driver (or if you have a car you can cut down the costs of your travel by taking passengers) who has to make a long-distance journey. In Spain there are various offices of Iberostop España, which forms part of International Eurostop (an organization with seventy-five offices in eight countries) based in Brussels. For a small fee and on presentation of two passport photographs you can join this association, which will find you lifts. Once a member all you have to do is

telephone one of the offices (they speak German,
English and Spanish in the Spanish offices) three or
four days before your journey and tell them where
you want to go – either within Spain or internationally. They will attempt to find someone making
that journey and you will only have to pay part of
the petrol costs. If you are a member with a car you
can telephone to say where you are travelling and
they will look for passengers.

There are various offices in Spain:

Barcelona	Tel: 93-246 6908 (10.00–15.00)
Granada	Tel: 958-29 29 20 (10.00–20.00)
Malaga	Tel: 952-254 4584 (16.00–18.30)
Seville	Tel: 954-38 82 80 (10.00–20.00)
Lloret de Mar	Tel: 972-36 83 01 (10.00–14.00)

**Peninsula–
island travel**

The alternative to flying from mainland Spain to
the Canaries or the Balearics is to take a ferry.
Trasmediterranea is the largest company and offers
services from several peninsular ports to the islands.
For example you can sail from Barcelona to the
Balearics, from Cadiz to the Canaries and to Palma
de Mallorca and from Valencia to the Balearics. All
of the ships which operate on these routes can carry
cars, and passenger accommodation consists of either
reclining seats or various sorts of cabin. On board
services include bars, restaurants, shops and even
discotheques. The crossing from Barcelona to Palma
takes eight hours, from Barcelona to Ibiza between
nine and ten hours and from Cadiz to Las Palmas
thirty-six hours. Don't forget when you plan your
journey that local time in the Canaries is one hour
behind peninsular time, though the Balearics are in
the same time zone as the peninsula. Trasmediterranea
have an agent in London (see below), where the
timetable and prices can be obtained and advance
bookings made before you leave for Spain. Outside
Britain, see your local travel agents for information.

You can also cross to Ibiza from Denia, some
43 km north of Alicante. The company FLEBASA
has a car ferry service every day in the high season,
with a morning service which leaves Denia early

(usually at 07.30) and takes three hours to cross to San Antonio on Ibiza, and an evening service (usually at 22.00) which takes five hours. FLEBASA is a much smaller company than Trasmediterranea and has no representatives outside Spain, but their local office address is included below.

There are good and frequent inter-island services in the Canaries by air or sea. Iberia operates regular services from Tenerife to Lanzarote/Arrecife, to Las Palmas, to Santa Cruz de la Palma and to Fuerteventura. Trasmediterranea has a hydrofoil and ferry service between all the islands, details of which can be found in their main timetable, but there are other companies too, such as Ferry Gomera which sails between Tenerife and La Gomera, and Jetfoil which runs a hydrofoil service between Tenerife and Las Palmas. Details of the various services can always be found at the local tourist offices or travel agents.

Peninsula–North African coast

If you are staying near Algeciras it is well worth considering a day-trip across the Straits to Morocco to plunge into the bustle of an Arabic world, if only for a few hours. The ferry from Algeciras to Tangiers takes two and a half hours but there is a much faster service from Tarifa, 20 km further west. From Tarifa the hydrofoil takes 40 minutes and the ferry 75 minutes. Tickets for this service can be bought on the day at the ports.

If you go on your own just for the day it is probably best to save time and take a taxi from the port to the *medina*, the old centre of the city, where you will find the most wonderful aromatic food shops and stalls, tea shops (where you ought to try the local mint tea with pastries) and restaurants. You will also find plenty of handicraft shops where you can bargain for beaten metalwork, leather goods and woven woollen blankets, hangings and carpets. Spanish currency is generally readily accepted in most places which are used to tourists. It is worth thinking about paying for an inclusive day-tour from Spain (bookable through travel agents) because this will give you a local Moroccan guide, a coach tour that takes you to various parts of the city and usually to a high viewing point to see where the Mediterranean and the Atlantic join, a walking tour of the old centre of Tangiers, and lunch.

Whether you go on your own or on a tour do not be surprised if, when disembarking at Tangiers, the Moroccan police take your passport. Instead of stamping it and returning it they usually keep the passports on the ship and give you a ticket which you use to collect yours when you embark for the return journey.

Once again, Trasmediterranea offers various services to the Spanish enclaves on the North African coast – from Malaga and Almeria to Melilla and from Algeciras to Ceuta. If you are taking a car the cheapest way to do it is to cross to Ceuta and enter Morocco from there.

Ferry addresses

Trasmediterranea
Melia Travel Ltd
12 Dover Street
London W1X 4NS
UK
Tel: 01-409 1884

FLEBASA
Estación Marítima
Denia
Spain
Tel: 578-40 11

Local journeys

Underground railway (metro)

Madrid and Barcelona have *metros* (open 06.00–01.30) which cover most of the centre of the cities. Tickets are very cheap, about 50 pesetas for a single journey to any station in the system. You can also buy cheaper books of ten tickets or a tourist card (*Metrocard*) for three or five days which allows unlimited use of the *metro*. You are asked to keep your ticket while you are travelling but in fact you only need to use it to get into the system, as it is not collected when you leave.

Valencia has recently opened seven new stations

to form part of a small underground system. This is actually a connection of several previously existent narrow gauge lines in the centre of the city and is very restricted.

Bus services within the larger towns and cities are *Bus* frequent and the tickets are very cheap, but it is often difficult, if you do not know the city, to find your way about, so it is worth considering a taxi. If you have to ask for the bus stop it is a *parada de autobuses.*

Taxis are usually reasonably cheap within cities. *Taxi* Licensed taxis will have meters so you can see exactly how much you are paying, but you may pay a supplement for luggage. If you travel beyond the city limits (and these points are marked at the side of the main road with a sign saying *limite taxi*) you will certainly have to pay a higher fare, so if your journey is to be a long one then it is best to ask about the price before setting off. Sometimes taxi drivers try to get away without putting on the meter; tell them to turn it on. Do beware of unlicensed taxis, which often operate at airports, railway stations and bus stations, and the drivers of which will offer to find hotel accommodation for you if you look like a tourist with luggage. There is usually no need to take an unlicensed taxi, but if you do then negotiate the fare before you start.

Driving

Having a car with you in Spain obviously gives you the greatest freedom of travel and allows you to explore areas where lack of good public transport makes access difficult. Spanish roads are rarely congested, except for the main roads from the coast to the nearby large cities at the end of the weekend, and driving outside the main urban centres is usually pleasant and relaxed once you have become accustomed to the bad surface on many minor roads. However, driving in the cities could not really be described as relaxed, though it is a delight for those who would drive with panache.

Documents   To drive in Spain you need either the pink EEC driving licence or your current national driving licence accompanied by an International Driving Permit. In the UK, this can be obtained for a small fee from your local AA or RAC office; those outside the UK should apply to a national automobile association in their own country. Although Spanish regulations state that one must be in possession of an International Driving Permit it is rarely asked for, certainly not when hiring a car in Spain. If you are stopped by the police on the road and they do ask for an international licence they often look for a registration number on the permit, and it is useful to type your driving licence number onto the cover.

If you have your own car with you, you must make sure that you are fully insured, and you should ask your insurance company for an International Green Card and Bail Bond (the latter is a special insurance against your car and goods being impounded in case of an accident). The AA and RAC offer a comprehensive insurance package for both members and non-members. This is particularly useful because it means that you are entitled to make use of the International Touring Alliance (AIT) service for motorists; the Spanish club member is the RACE (Real Automovil Club de España).

Documents, passport, driving licence, Green Card and registration book should be carried at all times when you are driving because if you are stopped by the police they will ask for these. You need not have committed any infringement to be stopped by the police, for the *guardia civil* (the paramilitary police who patrol the highways in cars and on motorbikes) quite often stop the traffic simply to check documents.

Preparations for travel

If you are travelling in your own car through Spain then it is wise to carry certain things with you. Officially you should have a sticker identifying your country (for example a GB sticker if you are in a British car), a red warning triangle to set up in case of an accident or breakdown, a spare headlight and spare light bulbs. Small items such as a fan belt, fuses, hoses, points, distributor cap and perhaps an emergency plastic windscreen save an irritating waste of time looking for spares.

Maps

There are many different sorts which can be bought prior to travelling. Michelin produce a map of the main roads (with a scale of 1 cm to 10 km) and a set of seven detailed maps which cover all of the peninsula (on a scale of 1 cm to 4 km).

A particularly good book of maps which is available in Spain is that published by the Ministry of Public Works (MOPU – *Ministerio de Obras Públicas y Urbanismo*). It is called *España Mapa Oficial de Carreteras*, costs around £6.00 and can be bought at most bookshops (*librerías*). Not only does it have clear, detailed maps of all roads, with petrol stations marked, but it also has some street plans, an alphabetic list of all towns and villages, emergency telephone numbers and other information which is useful to tourists and drivers. It is well worth buying.

Campsa, one of the main petrol companies, also produces a book of maps, *Guía Campsa*; this gives detailed road maps, but these are not as clear as those in the MOPU guide. What this book of maps does have, though, is a guide, by city, to over 800 hotels and restaurants throughout Spain. Rather charmingly, at the end Campsa rates the major restaurants, their quality being marked by one, two, three or four petrol pumps. The guide also includes useful information such as local Red Cross points and information offices.

Intercity driving

Spain is not well served with motorways (*autopistas*) and those which do exist, except for a few sections, charge a toll which is quite high. There are motorways entering the country from France into the Basque country and Catalonia; leaving Madrid; along the Costa Brava to just south of Valencia; from Zaragoza to the Mediterranean coast; from Zaragoza to Logroño (continuing up to Bilbao and Santander) and Pamplona; a short section from La Coruña going south; between Oviedo and León; and two from Seville, one to the Atlantic coast at Huelva and the other to Cadiz. The advantage of the motorways is that there is far less traffic on them than on the national roads (the tolls see to that), the trucks seem to avoid them and you can save on petrol by steady driving. Given the low density of motorway traffic it is generally true that there are fewer police patrols. The sign for a motorway (see illustration) is a large, square, blue and white one, with a flat bridge over a road and the words *autopista* and *peaje* (toll). If you do not wish to enter the motorway look out for the alternative routing which will be indicated. When you enter the motorway you will be given a ticket at the first booth and you pay when you leave the motorway or go onto the next section.

The majority of main trunk roads are N (national) roads. The important national roads are indicated by white lettering on a red background with the number in roman numerals after the N, for example 'N IV'. Other main roads are indicated by a white N and the number in arabic numerals (for example 'N 401') on a red background. Local main roads have a white C and a number on a green background, and the smallest roads (byroads) have a white LC and number on a yellow background. The major national roads are usually quite good, and have certainly improved considerably in the last few years, but many still seem to suffer from the fact that ill-prepared surfaces result in the asphalt being squeezed to the side; something which can make for bumpy driving. The smaller roads require concentration when driving in order to avoid the potholes and to cope generally with the poor surface, but if you want to see the more remote parts of Spain then these are the roads for you.

Spain adheres to the International Highway Code. *Regulations*
You must of course drive on the right and you must give way to traffic from the right. Safety belts must be used outside the city limits; there are signs (black and white with a seated figure and safety belt) at the side of the road to tell you that the use of seat-belts is obligatory from that point. It is probably safer to use belts at all times, although if you are travelling with Spaniards they will find this most odd and they will unfasten theirs as soon as they enter a town. They seem to find the regulation both irksome and a violation of their right to decide how to drive; the willingness to wear belts when it is not obligatory smacks somewhat of wimpishness.

Despite the fact that you will see many motor-cyclists, especially in towns, without crash helmets, it is compulsory to wear them whatever capacity motorcycle you have.

On motorways (*autopistas*) the speed limit is 120 km *Speed limits*
an hour (about 75 mph), on main roads with two or more lanes 100 km (62 mph), on other main roads 90 km (56 mph) and on urban roads 60 km (37 mph). Of course these general limits may be reduced in certain circumstances, so look out for signs. Fines (*multas*) for infractions vary between about 1000 pesetas for 10 km per hour over the limit and 8000 pesetas for 40 km over. Spanish police use radar to catch speeding drivers. If you find the cars coming towards you are flashing their lights this usually

indicates a police checkpoint or the fact that they have a speed trap in operation; be warned.

One section of the *guardia civil*, the paramilitary police who normally wear the distinctive green uniform and shiny black tricorn hat, patrols the roads outside the city limits. Their cars and Landrovers are green and white and they also patrol on motorbike. If you see one on his bike there will be another close by, for *guardia civiles* always work in pairs – hence their nickname '*la pareja*' ('the couple'). If you have committed an infringement and are stopped by the police, claiming ignorance of the law or lack of Spanish is no guarantee that you will not be fined, but if you adopt a politely apologetic manner this will certainly help smooth your dealings with them.

Road signs Spanish road signs are international and thus fairly obvious. Certain Spanish expressions, though, are important to know: *ceda el paso* (give way), *peligro* (danger), *paso prohibido* (no entry), *dirección única* (one way), *desvio* (diversion), *obras* (road works), *estacionamiento prohibido* (parking prohibited), *escalón lateral* (a drop at the edge of the road). For other signs see the illustrations.

Traffic lights These can be disconcerting because not all of them
(semáforos) go through amber between go and stop, although, just to add to the anarchic fun of driving, some do. Spanish drivers often race through on amber, so do look to see if the car behind is close; the driver may expect you to go through and consequently be ready to cross with you! If you are the first car in line at red traffic lights be ready to go quickly if you do not want to be subjected to irate hooting. Drivers become particularly impatient at traffic lights, and it is often said that the shortest measurable unit of time in Spain is that between the instant when the traffic lights go green and when the driver at the end of the queue starts hooting. Two flashing amber lights, either on a post at the side of the road or on a cable above the road, are a warning and usually indicate that you are approaching traffic lights.

In many cities you may well be confronted with windscreen washers working at traffic lights. These

Drinking water

National monuments

Picturesque view

Tourist information centre

No overtaking

No parking in direction of arrow

No parking in direction of arrow

Parking forbidden on even days of the month

Parking forbidden on odd days of the month

Sharp drop

Dangerous situation

Give way

Change of direction (i.e. you can cross the carriageway)

End of motorway

Centro Ciudad
City centre

Motorway (normally toll)

Ronda
Ring road

Some important road signs

people descend on the first couple of cars stopped at traffic lights and start to wash the windscreen for money. It is almost impossible to stop them performing this 'service' (which is hardly a service because they only have a few moments to work and often leave the glass more smeared than when they started); they certainly do not stop when you tell them 'No thank you' and you will probably end up by paying a few pesetas – 25 pesetas is plenty. Some Spaniards commented to me that it was worth paying so that these people did not become unpleasant and threaten to break the glass; a threat which is sometimes made.

Overtaking   The same rules, road markings and signs which apply in Britain and elsewhere also apply in Spain (and see the illustration). While overtaking in a right-hand drive car does not present too many problems when attempting to get past a car (especially when you have a passenger who can tell you whether it is safe), this is sometimes difficult when you are attempting to get past a truck and your vision is obscured. Most Spanish truck-drivers, however, are helpful and will indicate, by signalling with their right-hand indicator, when it is safe to pass (be careful, though, that they are not making a right-hand turn). The use of the left-hand indicator means 'do not pass'. At night they will often keep their headlights on full until you draw level with them and will then dip them. A hoot of appreciation from you is a suitable response.

A cautionary   Many Spanish drivers, particularly motorcyclists,
note   apparently feel that the obligation to drive or ride with lights on at dusk or even in the dark is an unacceptable imposition on their personal freedom. It is all too easy to come suddenly upon a motorcyclist with no lights or reflector panel, so caution is needed when driving at night.

Another potentially dangerous time in rural areas is when people are returning from the fields. Mopeds, small motorbikes and trail bikes have often replaced living beasts of burden and it is common to encounter dozens of these unlit machines spread out along the highway hurtling towards the nearest village. Not all mules and donkeys have been done away with, though, and in many areas it is possible to come across these ambling along in the dusk. The other obstacle to look out for is the odd flock of sheep wandering down or crossing the highway.

City driving

This can be apparently chaotic and certainly unnerving if you do not know where you are going. Spanish drivers seem to delight in frequent lane changes in order to gain even a little distance, and if there are two lanes for traffic marked out they are usually able to form three lines of cars. It does seem that the painted lines are taken as no more than helpful suggestions as to possible traffic configurations put there by the authorities. To make sure that others are aware of their intentions, especially if they are crossing lanes or pushing in, drivers will usually hang their left arm out of the window and wave their hand up and down. You can do this as well, but if you are driving a right-hand drive car it will not signal anything more than good intentions because you will be doing it on the wrong side, and you will achieve little more than almost shaking hands with the driver coming across from the right. If you have a passenger let them do it; it will allow them to feel that they are participating in the adventure, although trying to read a map and street signs in swiftly moving traffic will probably be adventure enough.

Two signs that will be useful as you attempt to negotiate your way around a city are those for a ringroad (*ronda*) and for the centre of the city (*centro ciudad*).

Parking

Parking can be somewhat difficult in Spanish cities (especially the smaller ones) because of the scarcity of custom-built car parks. The signs you are looking for are either a white P on a square blue sign or the words *aparcamiento* or *estacionamiento*, both of which mean parking. The illuminated sign *libre* outside a multistorey car park means 'free' in the sense that there are spaces available, and *completo* means you are out of luck.

It is much more fun to attempt to park in the streets, where parking is an anarchic art. Spaniards quite happily double park, park on the pavement and generally squeeze their cars into places that most orderly-minded tourists would not think of, or dare to try if they did think of them. Double parking is quite common but if you do it don't forget to leave your handbrake off and the car out of gear, so that it can be moved if necessary. It is important here to emphasize that this is not a joke; double parking can only work as a 'system' if the double parked cars can be moved along by the drivers who are blocked in. If you find that you have been blocked in by someone who has double parked alongside you or behind you, first try to push the offending vehicle out of the way. If that doesn't work the next move is to stand beside your car and lean on the horn, wait a while and lean on it again; keep repeating the process. People will look out of shops, bars and flats to see if it is their car which is causing the problem. If, after ten minutes, this hasn't worked it is best to retire to a bar and have a calming beer.

If you are attempting to squeeze into a small parking space it seems that the 'proper' method is to reverse very gently until you touch the car behind and then repeat the process in first gear until you bounce into the car in front; you will then be parked.

Parking meters   These are a fairly recent introduction in the larger cities and seem to be an attempt to impose some sort of order on the chaotic parking which often restricts the flow on main streets. Parking zones controlled by meters are marked by blue lines on the road itself, and close by there will be an orange meter for that particular zone. Parking costs 50 pesetas per hour (although you can pay for smaller units of time) and there is a maximum time of two hours. Put the money in the machine and press the yellow button for the ticket, which must then be displayed in the car. The authorities are particularly generous to drivers who overstay the limit and if you are fined you may cancel this by putting 200 pesetas in the machine, turning the black dial and either taking this ticket to the traffic warden, or displaying it in the car window, within an hour of being fined.

Parking meters operate Mondays to Fridays between 09.00 and 14.00 and between 17.00 and 20.00, and on Saturdays between 08.00 and 14.00. On Sundays and public holidays you do not have to pay.

Where not to park The main no-parking signs are round, red-edged signs with a blue background and a red diagonal line; the white arrow on the sign indicates the direction in which parking is prohibited. A similar sign with two red diagonal lines indicates no parking in any direction (see illustrations). Parking is also prohibited at any point at which the curb is broken to form an entrance to a garage in a commercial or residential street.

Be especially careful not to park in a zone where there is a sign of a hoist on the back of a truck towing a car and the words *retirada grua* (tow away). Cars found parked here are likely to be taken to the police car pound and it costs a considerable amount to reclaim them. If you are unfortunate enough to have your car towed away you will have to ask someone, preferably a policeman, for the *deposito de coches de la comisaría* (police car pound). The costs for retrieving your car can be as much as £35.00. In some cities the police are using wheel clamps (a *cepo*, literally and functionally a trap or snare) and again you will have to ask for the *comisaría* to sort this out.

In many places there will be someone to 'help' you park and 'look after' your car when you leave it; these are the *guardacoches* (parking attendants). Usually they are not operating in any official capacity (although some are, and they usually issue tickets); they are simply men who have bought themselves a peaked cap and attempt to eke out a living by controlling a part of a street or a square where people park. It only costs a few pesetas (usually 25 pesetas) to park on their patch and although there is no guarantee that your car will not be broken into, it does reduce the risk. Thefts from foreign registered cars or cars from another province have, unfortunately, become very common in Spain, particularly in the large cities and tourist resorts, and if you encounter a *guardacoches* attempting to tell you that you cannot park in a place where there is obviously space it is because he is worried about being held responsible for a car being broken into.

Theft from parked cars   The Spanish police are most concerned about the number of thefts from cars. Seville in particular has a terrible reputation for this, and the police do continually warn tourists not to leave things in their cars. As their information sheets warn, 'Your car is not a safe.' Theft of car radios is particularly popular in Seville and other large cities, and you will see many drivers who, to avoid this, carry their radios with them after they have parked.

Obviously it is difficult or at least inconvenient if you are touring in a car to ensure that it is empty every time you park, but you really should be very careful. As soon as you arrive at your hotel remove *everything* from the car and the boot if the hotel does not have a lock-up garage. It is not safe to lock your luggage in the boot because if there is nothing in the rest of the car this is the first place a thief will look, and car boots are easily opened with a small crowbar. Personally I always leave the boot of my own car empty and open (although car-hire companies ask you not to do so) because this does avoid the damage if someone puts a crowbar to it, and foreign registered cars are rarely stolen. Unfortunately it really is a case of removing *everything*; I have seen a car with the side window smashed at night just to get a packet of cigarettes left on the dashboard.

This negative note is not to imply that Spain is a nation of thieves or that there are thousands of people waiting to steal from tourists, but if you exercise caution so that you do not fall foul of the thieves who do exist, you will not suffer experiences which might then influence how you feel about the country. If you are unfortunate enough to suffer a theft from your car you will need to report this to the police (see 'Emergencies' for the procedure).

Petrol

Although there are three main petrol companies, CAMPSA, REPSOL and CEPSA, there is no competition in terms of prices (although this will change in 1992) because these are fixed by the government and apply nationally. There is therefore no need for, or use in, driving to look for cheap fuel. Filling stations are *gasolineras* and, except in the largest cities, are rarely to be found in the centre of town; they are usually located on the main roads leading out of town and of course on the highways themselves. Petrol stations are normally open from 07.00 until 22.00 or 23.00, and some are open 24 hours a day. If a station is closed there will usually be a notice indicating the nearest 24-hour one.

There are two main grades of petrol, *Super* (97 octane), which is the nearest equivalent to British 4-star, and *Normal* (92 octane) equivalent to British 2/3-star. Petrol stations also sell diesel (*gasóleo*). Most stations are not self service and the usual way to ask for petrol is in terms of pesetas – *'Deme mil [dos mil] pesetas por favor'* ('Give me 1000 [2000] pesetas' worth, please') – or to ask for the tank to be filled – *'Llenelo por favor'* ('Fill it up, please') or simply *'Lleno por favor'* ('Full, please'). If you need oil you should ask for *aceite*, and distilled water for batteries is *agua destilada*.

Although petrol stations often have toilet facilities (*servicios*) and some sell bags of ice-cubes, do not expect to find soft drinks (though there are a growing number with vending machines which have cold drinks), confectionery, snacks and cigarettes. This is no real hardship because you are never likely to be far from a roadside bar where you can eat, drink and have a break from driving.

Breakdowns

If you break down on the road you should display your red warning triangle some 50 m behind the car. If you are on anything but the most isolated roads it will not be long before the *guardia civil* arrive, and if it looks impossible to fix the car there it is possible to ask them to arrange for someone to come and tow you to a garage (*un taller*); '*Necesito una grua*' ('I need a tow') should do the trick. If you do not have the insurance cover which includes breakdown then this will have to be paid for.

Once again, if you have the Berlitz or similar phrase book you will find a detailed section for dealing with car problems, but a few useful words and phrases are:

El coche no arranca.	The car won't start.
Tengo un pinchazo.	I have a puncture.
No funcciona . . . (point to the part).	The . . . (point) doesn't work.
Hay algo estropeado con . . . (point to the part).	There is something wrong with . . . (point to the part).

Bateria	Battery
Radiador	Radiator
Distribuidor	Distributor
Platinos	Contact points
Bujías	Spark plugs
Bobina	Ignition coil
Fusible	Fuse
Bombillas	Bulbs
Correa de ventilador	Fan belt
Neumático	Tyre
Cámara	Inner tube
Tubo de escape	Exhaust pipe
Repuestos or *recambios*	Spare parts

Spanish car mechanics tend to do much more than change parts; they actually attempt to repair them, and often come up with ingenious solutions to problems if the necessary spare part is not available. The other good news is that the labour costs are nowhere near as high as in Britain. Punctures are usually fixed with little waiting and if you do not want to pay for a new tyre they will plug the hole and put in an inner tube.

Accidents   If you have a minor accident involving another car and there is no injury to driver or passengers, it is usually fairly easy to resolve the problem by exchanging names, addresses and insurance details. The police do not need to be involved so long as there is agreement between the drivers involved. If, however, there is an argument or it is a major crash or there are injuries, then the police will necessarily become involved and will collect all details for an official statement called an *atestado*; the process will develop a momentum of its own without your being able to do very much about it.

The most important thing is to attempt to remain calm, see that the injured are dealt with and try to get as many details as possible; and that includes a sketch or photograph of the cars on the road, and names and addresses of witnesses if there are any. If things become serious or complicated it is best to attempt to get in contact with your nearest consulate (see 'Consular offices in Spain' for a list of addresses) to ask for advice.

Money matters

Currency There are no subdivisions of the Spanish peseta, which makes handling money quite easy. There are coins of 1 (virtually useless), 5, 25, 50, 100 and 200 pesetas (these are about the same size as a 5 peseta, so be careful not to pass them as such) as well as the new 500 pesetas (which looks somewhat like a smaller, gold-coloured version of the British 50 pence coin). Notes are for 100 (becoming rarer as they are withdrawn from circulation), 500, 1000, 2000, 5000 and 10,000 pesetas.

When you ask the price of an item it will be given to you as a simple figure, such as *dos cientos* ('two hundred') or *ciento veinte* ('one hundred and twenty'). There are numbers and parts of numbers which are tricky to catch, for example the difference between 60 (*sesenta*) and 70 (*setenta*), and those numbers which feature fives, such as *quinentas cincuenta y cinco* (555). The only other term you might hear, especially from older people and in markets, is *duro*, which is five pesetas. You might, for example, be asked if you have *cinco duros* (25 pesetas) in change. A *duro* is not technically a coin but just a way of referring to units of five pesetas.

Changing money Travellers in Spain can use travellers' cheques, most international credit cards, Eurocheques and Girobank cheques/Postcheques. All of these, with the exception of Girobank Postcheques, can generally be used in shops, garages, hotels and restaurants, but it is usually best to ask whether they can be used, especially if you are in smaller towns or villages and the establishment does not have credit card/travellers' cheques signs posted on the door.

If you are staying in a larger hotel there are quite often facilities for changing money, and although the commission rate will probably be higher than that of a bank the advantage is that you don't have to go looking for a bank and then wait to change your money. In hotels you can often change money when banks are not open, which is particularly useful if you urgently need money in the afternoon or on a Sunday. If you are really desperate it is sometimes possible to walk into a large hotel and change money, but they may well ask if you are registered there.

The usual way to change money is in a bank which displays a sign saying *CAMBIO*. Most banks are open to the public between 09.00 and 14.00 Mondays to Fridays, but there are some which open at 08.30. On Saturdays they are open between 09.00 and 12.30, except during the summer months (mid-June until the end of September).

Be prepared for a wait in most banks because the person who handles the paperwork for the transaction is not usually the person who gives out the money, and in some banks the transaction is checked by yet another person. At least you have a chance to observe an example of Spanish bureaucracy at work. Once in the bank, look for a counter which displays the *CAMBIO* sign and ask if you can change the cheque – '*¿Puedo cambiar este cheque, por favor?*' – or say that you would like to change a cheque – '*Quisiera cobrar este cheque, por favor.*' You will need to present your passport with the cheques or foreign notes which you wish to change. Having completed and signed (you will be asked for your *firma*) for this part of the transaction you will be given a copy of the exchange and directed to the cash desk, the *caja* – usually that part of the bank protected by thick glass. When it is your turn to be attended to, hand in your copy of the form and you will be given your money and a stamped receipt.

It is worth noting that there are various commission fees charged for changing money. The rate for foreign notes is usually 2 per cent, with a minimum charge of 250 pesetas. For travellers' cheques the same 2 per cent is charged, again with the same minimum of 250 pesetas, and there is a bank handling fee of 0.15 per cent or a minimum of 100 pesetas. It is really not worth regularly changing very small amounts of money, for you will have to pay the minimum fee each time.

Eurocheques are not subject to either a commission or bank handling fee. The great advantage of these cheques is that you simply write the cheque (in English, putting the currency symbol 'Ptas' in the appropriate box) for the amount you require, up to an amount of 20,000 pesetas (the present limit), and that is the amount you actually receive. As Eurocheques are a fairly recent phenomenon (at least in comparison with travellers' cheques) some smaller banks might say that they cannot cash them even though they have the Eurocheque sign displayed. This is usually because they are not sure how to handle them and they will direct you to a larger branch. In some towns and villages well off the normal tourist routes, bank assistants become disconcerted when confronted by Eurocheques and by the large manual they must consult in order to understand how to process them, and you must wait patiently as they consult with various colleagues, fill in numerous bank forms and copy down every possible number to be found on your passport, cheque card and cheque. In such banks they will sometimes actually charge a 1 per cent or 2 per cent commission, because that is what they are used to doing. You will need a good level of Spanish in order to tell them that they should not do this, and even then you risk them saying that they cannot cash the cheque. If you really do need the money it is worth paying – a small price for the experience of watching others coping with Europe. Similarly these cheques are sometimes refused in restaurants where staff are not quite sure how to deal with them.

Eurocheques are also useful in that, with a cheque card and knowing your PIN number, money can also be obtained from automatic cash dispensers outside banking hours. You should look for *TELE-BANCO* dispensers, which are easily identifiable by their yellow and blue stripes and which usually carry the Eurocheque sign. This facility is available at hundreds of banks across mainland Spain and the islands, and a full list can be obtained from the bank where you get your Eurocheques.

If you have a Girobank current account and cheque card then you will be able to cash cheques in post offices – *correos*. The counter which deals with such transactions is usually identified with a sign saying *caja postal de ahorros* or *reintegros*, and the process is similar to that described for cashing Eurocheques. You may write a cheque up to an equivalent of £100 in pesetas (the leaflet which comes with the cheques tells you the maximum in pesetas which can be drawn on a cheque) and you are not charged a commission. In post offices you are not usually sent to another counter to receive the cash; the clerk who carries out the transaction also pays you. Some smaller post offices may not offer this service and those which do usually have the counter open between 08.00 and 14.00 Mondays to Fridays. These cheques cannot be used in hotels, shops or restaurants.

Out of hours

Travellers' cheques can be cashed at many travel agents outside normal banking hours. This service is also available at the department store El Corte Ingles, branches of which can be found in major cities throughout Spain.

Cash can also be obtained on the presentation of a credit card, such as Visa or Access, at a bank. If you have your PIN number you can also get cash at any automatic cash dispenser which displays a picture of your credit card.

Import restrictions

The latest official information is that you may import an unlimited quantity of pesetas, but if the amount exceeds 100,000 you are advised that it is best to declare it so as to avoid problems when leaving the country. Similarly there is no limit to the amount of foreign currency you may import, but should this exceed a value of 500,000 pesetas it is best to declare it when entering. A non-resident may export 100,000 pesetas or the amount which was declared on entering the country, whichever may be the greater.

Communicating: telephones and letters

Telephones There are several places from which local, national and international calls can be made. The simplest way is to look for one of the aluminium and perspex telephone boxes (*una cabina*) which are to be found in the street. The vandalizing of telephone boxes seems not be a vice which has found much appeal in Spain so it is fairly easy to find one which works. *Cabinas* accept 5, 25 and usually 100 peseta coins (some of the older ones still accept 50 peseta coins) and although it is possible to make direct-dial international calls from them you will need a good supply of coins. European calls are manageable in terms of the number of coins necessary but, for example, transatlantic calls are barely feasible.

Money is introduced into the machine by way of a slide on the top of the apparatus. Do not try to force the money in; when there is a reply from the number you are calling the first coin will automatically fall in and the others will follow when necessary. Some of the more modern telephones have a slot for the money and an illuminated panel to tell you how much you have put in and how much remains during the conversation. Unused coins will be returned with this sort of machine. Do not press the button to the left of the dial (unless instructed to do so by an operator) as you may lose any money you have put in the machine.

For a local call you simply put two 5 peseta coins on the slide and dial the number. If you are dialling a number which is outside the province (Spanish towns have a provincial code, not an individual dialling code number) you will need to use the code number, which will be found on the information sheet in the *cabina*. For a long-distance number it is best to have several 25 peseta coins ready. Calling internationally from a *cabina* is easy – for example if you want to dial a British number you must dial the international number (07), wait until you hear the long, continuous tone, then dial 44 for Britain, then the STD code minus the first 0 and then the subscriber number you require. International code numbers are also displayed in most *cabinas*. The period for cheap rate calls from Spain to other parts of Europe is from 22.00 until 08.00 the following morning. Reverse charge calls cannot be made from a *cabina* because the operator will need to be able to call you back.

If you wish to make a long-distance or international call and do not have sufficient coins then you must look for a telephone office (*una telefónica*). The *telefónica* will have a reception desk from which you will be directed to a booth (also called a *cabina*) to make your call; you then pay at the reception desk. If the *telefónica* does not have direct-dial facilities you should write the number you want on a piece of paper and hand it to the receptionist; she will direct you to a booth once she has made the connection. Reverse charge calls (*una llamada cobro revertido*) can be made at a *telefónica*, but there is quite often a delay on the connection if the receptionists are busy, because they themselves must wait to connect with an international operator. The *telefónica* will have a complete set of telephone books for all of Spain.

Many bars have a telephone for public use, but if there is not one immediately visible you can ask one of the bar staff for permission to use their telephone – '*¿Puedo usar el teléfono por favor?*' This will be an ordinary direct-dial telephone, connected to a control box which measures the call by units. When you have finished you will be charged for the units used, but the cost is higher than using a public telephone because there is an official percentage increase on the call.

If you are staying in a hotel you will obviously be able to use the telephone, but once again there is an increased charge for the call and this can sometimes be quite high.

If you wish to make a directory enquiry within the province dial 003; for national enquiries dial 009. These numbers tend to be very busy, but there is another way to get the information you require. In the *cabina* you will find a list of provincial codes. Select the code of the province you require and then dial that number plus 003, and you will get through to an operator within the province. For international enquiries dial 008. Unfortunately, except for international enquiries, you cannot expect the operator to speak English.

Letters In larger post offices (*casa de correos* or *oficina de correos*), which are usually open between 09.00 and 14.00, there will be various windows, each of which handles a different type of transaction; you should look for the one with the sign *venta de sellos* if you wish to buy stamps. The simplest way of buying stamps is to show the official the letters or cards and let him/her work out what stamps are necessary. The word for a letter is *una carta*, a post card is *una tarjeta postal* and 'by airmail' is '*por correo aéreo*'. If you need a letter sent by express mail the term is *urgente*, and if you need it recorded delivery the term is *certificado*. Stamps can also be purchased at *estancos*, the officially licensed tobacco shops, which are easily identified by their distinctive yellow and dark red paintwork and the similarly coloured sign saying *tabaco*. Stamps can also be purchased at the reception desk of hotels.

Letters can be posted within the post office itself or in the post boxes on the outside wall, and if there are several to choose from *extranjero* is the one for foreign letters, *provincia* for within the same province and *nacional* for other parts of Spain. Post boxes in the street are of a similar barrel shape to the British variety and they are coloured yellow with red stripes. The green, square boxes which you might see are only for the use of postal staff.

Receiving You can arrange to have mail sent to you c/o a post
mail office in Spain. Letters should be addressed to you at *lista de correos*, followed by the name of the town/

city and province. If you are expecting mail in one of the large cities such as Madrid or Barcelona then you should look for the main post office and within that for the window or counter labelled *lista de correos*. You will need to show your passport and pay a few pesetas for the service.

Coping with Spaniards

It is always dangerous to talk in terms of national character, an exercise which usually leads to superficial statements or at worst to misleading stereotypes. There are as many Spanish 'characters' or personalities as there are Spaniards. This notion of personality or character, however, is not simply a matter of individual psychology for there is a social and cultural dimension to it, and in this sense you might well be able to construct a general image of Spaniards as distinct from the French, the Americans or the British. Fascinating though it might be to attempt an analysis of what makes a Spaniard a Spaniard, all that can be offered here are a few comments about socializing and generally 'coping' with Spaniards. Even here the problem is difficult because of highly distinctive regional cultures and patterns of life which shape the way people are; for example Basques are different in some ways from Castilians, who are different from Catalans, who are different from Andalusians, who are different from Galicians, who are different from . . .

In terms of my personal experience (and from what I have understood of the experience of other foreigners in Spain) I have found that one important element of character you can usually rely on is Spaniards' innate and pervasive sociability and readiness to communicate. You only have to compare the discreet silences of a group of English people who do not know each other in a railway carriage and the friendly chatter which quickly develops among a similar group of Spanish travellers who are strangers to one another to see this notion in operation. Given that a good deal of social life is maintained *en la calle* (literally 'in the street' but in general referring to any public place, of which bars are particularly important), and given that Spaniards generally enjoy conversation, it is relatively easy for a visitor to make contact with them. Asking questions about local food and drink, what there is of interest to see or do in the town or village, how to get somewhere or how to get something done is likely to draw you into conversation with whomever is standing near you at the bar.

Although a foreigner (away from the areas of mass tourism) may well be stared at as an object of curiosity, it is easy to turn that to your advantage if you are willing to attempt to overcome the language barrier and begin even a simple conversation of odd phrases and expressive gestures. Visitors will not find the attitude, reputedly held by members of other nations, that if you cannot speak the language well you are not worth talking to. Spaniards are generally pleased when a foreigner makes an effort to speak their language, they are remarkably patient with someone who is trying to communicate and they listen carefully in an attempt to make sense of the mangled grammar and odd vocabulary. Exactly *how* you say it is less important than your *wanting* to say it – if you are willing to plunge in they will help you to swim.

Spaniards are generous with both their time and their economic resources; they have highly developed notions of host and guest and will readily invite you to join them in a drink. This open hospitality and curiosity with regard to strangers are well illustrated by a personal experience. On a drive to a remote village in Aragon with two English friends I stopped at a restaurant for lunch. There were few diners except for a large group of men who were obviously celebrating something important. After thirty minutes or so one of them came over to us and said that he and his friends were a group of wine producers who were celebrating the establishment of a co-operative; they had noticed that we were foreigners and hoped that their exuberance had not interrupted our meal. He then produced a bottle of champagne and a bottle of red wine and asked us to enjoy celebrating their good fortune. Later that evening in a restaurant in another village a waiter brought us coffees and brandies which we had not ordered – they had come, he said, from a group of men at the bar. This was an opening which allowed me to go to thank them and to explain why we were in the village, a conversation which resulted in us spending the night at a local festival with them.

To become a welcomed guest, even if it only lasts for an evening in a bar or a day in a local festival, is a most pleasant position to be in in Spain and your visit will certainly be the richer for it.

Children   If you are travelling with young children you should not worry that they will be regarded as a nuisance and you will find it even easier to meet Spaniards, for children in Spain are not creatures to be kept apart from adult socializing in bars and restaurants. They love to show off their own children and coo indulgently over them and those of others, and they are likely to do the same with yours – even more so if they are blond.

Greetings   The most common Spanish greetins are *Hola* (Hello) and *Buenos dias/tardes/noches* (Good morning/afternoon/evening), and it is a normal politeness to use these terms together when entering a bar or shop. If you are introduced to someone you have a choice of expressions, a choice which hinges on the appropriate level of familiarity or reserved politeness, depending on exactly to whom you are being introduced. If you are introduced to a previously unknown adult it is best to err on the side of formality, shake hands and say something simple such as '*Encantado*' or '*Con mucho gusto*' ('Pleased' or 'Delighted') or more fully '*Encantado de conocerle*' ('Pleased' or 'Delighted to meet you') or '*Mucho gusto conocerle*' ('Pleased to meet you'). When you shake hands on leaving you should say '*Adios*' ('Goodbye') and the same phrase.

You might also hear Spaniards saying '*Hola, como esta usted?*' ('Hello, how are you?') If you are asked how you are the standard response is '*Bien gracias*' ('Well, thank you'). If you are introduced to a young person such greetings might suggest that you are maintaining an unnecessarily formal distance, and '*Hola*' or '*Qué tal*' ('How are you') is a more normal greeting.

The 'rules' about greeting with a kiss on the cheek (some people kiss on both cheeks) are somewhat ambiguous in this changing society. The safest advice is to shake hands rather than kiss older women (or men if you are a woman), but it is usually quite acceptable for younger people, when they are presented to each other, to kiss on the cheeks. It should be noted, though, that this 'kiss' is the slightest of actions. Quite often lips do not even touch the skin but rather the people lean forward, touch cheek to cheek, and a very slight sound of a kiss is sent in the direction of the ear. The kissing of a woman's hand seems to be an outmoded courtesy except in high society or on very special occasions and you are unlikely to come across it.

How not to be a *giri*

The word *giri*, which seems to derive from *girigay*, meaning to speak an unintelligible gibberish, has gained popular usage, particularly in the south of Spain, to refer disparagingly to tourists or other foreigners living in Spain. *Giris* are the object of much humorous comment because of their 'strange' dress and behaviour (which of course really only consists in not doing what Spaniards would normally do) and the way in which their white skin is burned to a colour resembling freshly cooked lobster or prawns. Despite the many biting comments it should not be assumed that tourists will not be well treated in Spain, although the recent poster campaign by the government, consisting of humorous cartoons designed to encourage Spaniards to be pleasant to summer visitors, suggests that the relationship has not been as good as it could be. The real problem has been the loud, drunken and otherwise coarse and insensitive behaviour of many groups who visit Spain on package tours; behaviour which led the king himself to comment recently that Spain was not receiving the tourists which it deserved.

I met this funny bloke the other day who didn't speak English

Starting from the obvious point that if you are reading this book you are unlikely to be planning a holiday consisting of staggering from bar to bar wearing little more than shorts depicting the colours of your national flag and singing your favourite football chants, how do you avoid being treated as a *giri*? The answer is actually quite simple. Although it is impossible to avoid being labelled as a *giri* (Spanish friends of mine told me that their English mother, who had spent the best part of her life in Spain, was a *giri*), sensitivity to Spanish codes of dress and public behaviour will assure that you are not treated in anything but a hospitable manner.

The most important point to note is that items of clothing such as shorts and beachwear are not appropriate dress for being in urban areas, whether this be city, town or village. Neither is it acceptable for a man to walk in the streets without his shirt on. It is not that Spaniards are particularly prudish about the sight of bare flesh in itself, for they too will wear bikinis, skimpy swimming trunks and shorts on the beach or at the local swimming pool; the concern is where it is revealed. There is a complex code of public dress and behaviour concerned with what is appropriate on the beach or in the countryside and what is appropriate in the city. The urban centre is the place of formal, civilized behaviour, and dress which does not complement this is frowned on. The mere fact that you are correctly dressed and, as the Spanish would say, *sabe comportarse* (know how to behave) will encourage the locals to respond to you as an individual and not as a mere tourist.

Apart from the prejudice against uncivilized tourists the only real bias that certain visitors might encounter, particularly along the south coast, is that against the British with regard to the issues of Gibraltar and occasionally of the Malvinas/Falklands, but this rarely results in adverse treatment.

Beggars

Unfortunately people begging in the street and in bars are a common sight in Spain. If you do not want to give them money when approached you only need to respond with a polite but firm 'no'. In many parts of Spain, but particularly in the south, you may encounter gypsies begging or attempting to sell you carnations. If you do not want to buy anything but you allow them to thrust a flower on you it will be difficult to escape without considerable argument. It is best not to accept anything, even if you are told it is a gift (*un regalo*). Some people offer a service such as shoe shining instead of direct begging, and if you want your shoes cleaned it is best to agree a price beforehand.

**Getting
things done**

Spanish bureaucrats and other officials, in common
with those of other nations, when asked to render a
service often find it easier to say 'no' than to say
'yes' and then have to attend to the thing in question.
You should not be put off by this. Spaniards are in
general insistent in their demands in most contexts,
whether this be in a market, bar or government office
– there is considerable truth in the comment that
each Spaniard carries a copy of the Spanish constitution which has only one article, stating that 'I can
do what the hell I want'. Spaniards most certainly
do not easily accept 'no' for an answer, and you
should not either.

In any context when you really want something
or need something done which is being refused, it is
best to remain patient but keep at it (losing your
temper or becoming angry in such circumstances is
certainly counterproductive, because in a conflictive
situation the other person is not going to want to
back down), explain again what you need and ask if
there is some other way of achieving it. The trick is
to maintain a conversation, keep the bureaucrats'
attention on you, to get them to respond to you as
a person and not simply a problem and, if possible,
attempt to engage their interest in your problem.

So much in Spain is achieved through a network
of individual contacts and friends of friends that all
sorts of problems can be resolved through unofficial
channels. You cannot expect to buy yourself out of
difficulty or to have a problem solved, but things do
get done for friends, and if you can make a friendly
contact this will help.

Timekeeping

The laziness of Spaniards implied in the concept of
mañana, with its suggestion of putting things off
until the tomorrow which never comes, is an image
which has been imposed on Spain by outsiders and
bears little relation to reality; certainly Spaniards do
not express their approach to life in terms of
mañana. This said, however, there is something of an
unhurriedness in terms of precise timekeeping, and
I have often been told to be *tranquilo* with regard
to my concern with an English sense of punctuality.

Although this can be frustrating if you are hoping to meet somebody or waiting for an office or museum to be open at a precise time, it can also be to your advantage if you are a little late yourself.

Quarter hours have little relevance in terms of Spanish timekeeping and Spaniards find it a little strange for someone to suggest that they meet or be ready for something at, for example, 11.15 or 10.45. The period in Spanish timekeeping which can be confusing is *medio dia* (midday), which is not 12.00. If someone says they will meet you or call you *a medio dia* they are referring to lunch time, between 14.00 and 16.00. This certain looseness of timekeeping should not be assumed to apply to services such as trains, buses or planes, even though it is traditionally said that the only thing which begins on time in Spain is the bullfight.

Siesta

Although the size of cities (such that people cannot easily get from work to home and back in the afternoon break) and changing work hours is reducing the importance of the *siesta* (the afternoon sleep), in some parts of Spain it is still a common practice. It is best to expect very little activity between lunch time and about 16.30, when offices, public buildings and shops tend to be closed. The *siesta* is particularly important during the summer when many parts of Spain are blisteringly hot and the only sensible thing is to hide behind closed shutters. Taking a *siesta* also allows you to face the late Spanish nightlife somewhat refreshed.

Hotels and other accommodation

Hotels   There is a great range of hotels and similar accommodation, from the super-luxurious five-star to the humble *pension* and *fonda* (guesthouse or lodging house). All such establishments are government registered and inspected and their prices are also set by the government. It is usually easy to find hotel accommodation of some sort when you arrive in a town (except in popular coastal resorts or when the town is celebrating some major *fiesta*), but if you intend to stay in a quality hotel and you know when you will be there, then it is best to make reservations either by telephone or letter (see sample letter at the end of this chapter). If you contact a hotel of three, four or five stars you will be able to write in English and if you call there should be somebody who will speak it. If you do call, though, it is best to do so during the day or early evening, because at night the receptionist at smaller hotels is less likely to speak English. The two most comprehensive guides to Spanish hotels are the Red Michelin guide and the official *Gúia de Hoteles*, which is published by the Spanish Ministry of Tourism and is easily available from bookshops in Spain.

Because hotels and other places which offer accommodation are government regulated, they must fulfil certain requirements according to their star rating. Below is a list of the main facilities in terms of the rooms (there are other, more general requirements) which will be found in each category of hotel.

Five-star – airconditioning in all public rooms and bedrooms; central heating; all bedrooms have fully furnished bathrooms.
Four-star – airconditioning in all public rooms and bedrooms unless the local climatic conditions require

only central heating or refrigeration; 75 per cent of bedrooms have full private bathroom; the rest have shower, wash-basin, hot and cold water and WC.

Three-star – permanently installed heating; 50 per cent of bedrooms have full private bathroom; 50 per cent have showers, wash-basin, hot and cold water and WC.

Two-star – permanently installed heating; 15 per cent of bedrooms with full private bathroom; 45 per cent with shower, wash-basin, hot and cold water and WC; the rest with shower, wash-basin, hot and cold water and no WC; one common bathroom per seven rooms.

One-star – permanently installed heating; 25 per cent of bedrooms with wash-basin, shower, hot and cold water and WC; 25 per cent with shower, wash-basin and hot and cold water, no WC; the rest with wash-basin and hot and cold water; one common bathroom per seven rooms.

Hostels

The next general grade is that of *hostales* or *pensiones*, which can usually be defined by their signs, consisting of the letters HS or P on a blue background outside the establishment. These are usually more modest forms of accommodation but, like hotels, they are graded according to the facilities offered. It should be added here that because the star rating is based on facilities a two- or three-star hostel can be better in terms of furnishing than a low-rated hotel.

Three-star – permanently installed heating; 5 per cent of rooms with full bathroom facilities; 10 per cent with shower, wash-basin, hot and cold water and WC; 85 per cent with shower, hot and cold water; one common bathroom per eight bedrooms.

Two-star – permanently installed heating; all bedrooms with wash-basin and hot and cold water; one common bathroom per ten bedrooms.

One-star – all rooms with wash-basin and cold water; one bathroom per twelve bedrooms.

Guesthouses

The most basic form of accommodation (in the sense that rooms are likely to have only a simple bed and wash-basin) is to be found in *fondas* or *casas de huespedes*, which are both forms of guesthouse or lodgings. They can be identified by signs with the letters F or CH in white letters on a blue background, and are usually to be found in the older sections of towns.

Prices

Prices in all such establishments vary not only according to their category but also according to whether it is high, medium or low season. Prices will also rise during important local festivals. Low season is usually from 1 January until 25 March, mid-season from 4 April to 30 June and 1 November to 31 March and high season from 1 July to 31 October. The Easter period is also high season. It is worth noting that, because of their location and type of tourism, high season in the Canaries and in the mountain resorts (particularly where there is skiing) is in winter.

Wayside restaurants

Not only are there hotels in the towns but you will also find places for overnight stops on main roads. Many of the wayside restaurants, often called *ventas*, have accommodation which they advertise with the sign *camas* (beds). If you cannot see a sign but the establishment looks large enough to have rooms above the restaurant you can ask '*¿Hay camas?*' ('Are there beds?'). These places are useful if you are on a long drive and need a meal and an overnight stop and yet do not want to start searching in the nearest town or village.

Booking in

If you are interested in rooms at a particular hotel and the reception staff do not speak English you will need to find out whether they have rooms – '*¿Hay habitaciones?*' For an individual room you should ask for *una habitación individual*. You may well find that there are actually two single beds in the room, but you will only be charged the individual rate. If you intend to share a room you need *una habitación doble*, which will be a room with two single beds; if you want a double bed you should ask for *una habitación con cama matrimonial* (literally 'a room with a matrimonial bed'). It is rare in Spain these days for an unmarried couple to be refused a double room or a double bed but it does occasionally occur in smaller towns. A room with a bath is *una habitación con baño*, and one with a shower is *una habtiación con ducha*. Should you need to ask about them, sheets are *sabanas*, blankets are *mantas* and pillows *almohadas*.

In hotels with restaurants it is possible to ask for a full-board rate (*pensión completa*), but it is usually more interesting just to use your hotel as a base and explore what is on offer in the local restaurants. Except in the best hotels it is advisable to avoid the breakfast, which tends to consist of unappetizing rolls and mediocre croissant look-alikes. If you enjoy good coffee then certainly keep away from the set breakfast, where coffee tends to be semi-instant, made by the jugful and not very good. Spain has wonderful coffee, but head for a nearby bar to find it. In the bars you will also have the chance to try a range of local spreads on toasted rolls or bread (see the chapter on 'Restaurants and bars').

Having decided to take a room you will have to sign a registration document and give the receptionist your passport so that the details can be filled in for police registration. There is no need for your passport to be kept at reception; as soon as you have fully registered you can ask for it to be returned.

At the end of your stay you will be expected to check out by noon. In some hotels the price of the room already includes the government tax IVA, but if it does not this will be added to your bill – 6 per cent for all establishments with the exception of five-star hotels, where it is 12 per cent. Full details of the cost of the room, board and taxes will be displayed on an officially stamped notice in the room, usually on the door.

Hopefully you will have no need to complain about the service or facilities, but if you do and the problem is not resolved immediately, you have the right to ask for the *hojas de reclamaciones* or the *libro de reclamaciones* – official complaints books which are checked by a government official.

Paradores The Spanish tourist industry is justifiably proud of its unique network of hotels called *paradores*. These are hotels ranging from three- to five-star, the majority of which are restored and converted historic monuments.

A *parador* was originally an inn which offered lodging to, in the words of the Ministry of Tourism, 'more respected persons'. In 1926 the Marquis of Vega-Inclán, the Royal Tourist Commissioner, initiated a project to build a network of state *paradores*, the first of which was an inn for hunters and nature lovers in the Gredos mountains. From that beginning the project has developed and slowly built up a network of eighty-six *paradores*. The majority of the buildings are castles, monasteries, convents or palaces, and great care has been taken to preserve their decor and distinctive characteristics while converting them into high-quality modern hotels. Even the modern, purpose-designed *paradores* reflect regional styles and have unique decor and furnishing. You will rarely find bland or anonymous 'international' hotel styles in the *parador* chain. Not only do they emphasize regional styles in terms of decor but their restaurants also pride themselves on their regional cuisine and their regional wine list.

Travelling around Spain using *paradores* is undoubtedly a very special way of seeing the country, not only because of the quality of the hotels but also because many are located away from normal centres of mass tourism. As might be expected, though, this is not a particularly cheap experience. *Parador* reservations can be made directly through the central office in Madrid or, more easily, through their London or US agents (addresses below). If you write to the London agent requesting information you will be sent a very useful guide book, *Visiting the Paradores*, and a map, as well as a complete price list. The official UK representative for ATESA (car hire) also offers individually tailored 'fly and drive' tours which combine the services of Iberia, ATESA and the *parador* network.

Useful addresses Central de Reservas de Paradores
Veláquez 18

28001 Madrid
Spain
Tel: 1-4359700 or 4359744

Marsans Travel
205 East 42nd St
Suite 1514
New York, NY 10017
USA
Tel: 661-6565

Marsans Travel
1680 Michigan Avenue
Professional Tower
Suite 1140
Miami, Fl 33139
USA
Tel: 531-0144

Marsans Travel
3325 Wiltshire Blvd
Suite 508
Los Angeles, Cal 90010
USA
Tel: 738-8016

The official UK representative is:

Keytel International
402 Edgware Road
London W2 1ED
UK
Tel: 01-402 8182

Fly-drive schemes can be arranged through:

ATESA
7a Henrietta Place
London W1M 9AG
UK
Tel: 01-493 4934

Spain has hundreds of registered camp sites (*campings*) **Camping**
where you can pitch your tent or park a caravan.

These sites can be found close to major cities, in beach areas, by rivers and lakes and generally throughout the variety of landscapes of Spain.

As with hotels, the sites are subject to local government inspection, registration and price fixing, and they are classified as being first, second or third class. This classification is somewhat peculiar in that some second category sites offer as much as first category and, except in the most luxurious sites, the prices charged per car, tent and person vary only minimally. For example, two people with a tent and car might pay about 1400 pesetas in a first category site and 1140 at a second category. The total price charged for staying at a camp site is calculated per car/caravan or camper, per adult/child and per tent (here the price varies according to whether the tent is individual or family-sized). This price will include the use of all the main facilities; you might have to pay extra for hot showers (the cold ones and other washing facilities are free), but many sites offer these free too.

Considering the range of facilities offered by most sites, camping is a particularly good deal in Spain. The Ministry of Tourism and Spanish Camping Federation produce an indispensable guide to camp sites, *Gúia de Campings*, in which details of the prices per day and all the facilities are listed in a code which is explained bilingually. Most first category sites have showers, launderette facilities, bars, restaurants, first aid/medical facilities, shops (where you will be able to buy, among other things, camping gas cylinders), swimming pools, telephones, post box, safes for valuables, electric and water supply for caravans and a range of sporting facilities, as well as many other services. Second and third category sites should not automatically be regarded as necessarily inferior, for many will have almost the same facilities. The guide book also gives information as to the setting of the camp site, the nature of the terrain — what the natural vegetation is and whether the site is wooded, at the side of a river or lake or near the beach — as well as anything special which the site has to offer visitors.

Camp sites near the coast and in favourite tourist centres can become full in peak season, but it is possible to make reservations through the Spanish Camping Federation's main office in Madrid. This service is free, and they can also supply the guide book.

Although the International Camping Carnet, which can be obtained through British camping organizations (see addresses below), the AA or other national camping federations, is not necessary if you are using the registered sites, it can be useful sometimes. Officially this carnet is required if you want to camp away from such sites, and for off-site camping you do of course need the permission of the local landowner and also that of the local police. Off-site camping is permitted in Spain, but not in the mountains or on beaches, and you will notice that beach areas are often well patrolled by police.

Farmhouses

In recent years the Ministry of Tourism has put together a new scheme of holiday accommodation based on farmhouses and cottages (*casas de labranza*) throughout Spain. This scheme, little known among visitors to Spain, is not as extensive or developed as the *gîte* system in France, but there is a great range of accommodation to choose from.

Although these are houses of agriculturalists they are not necessarily out in the country – indeed, the majority are in villages. Government money has been given to agriculturalists to improve either their own home or a house which they own but do not use, in order to make it suitable for receiving tourists. This has had the effect of conserving and modernizing country dwellings and of offering the possibility of holidays away from the traditional centres of tourist concentration and away from normal hotels. The programme has carefully selected areas because of their natural beauty and for the services (and this includes sporting facilities) available in the locality.

What the scheme really offers is a chance to see, and to some extent share, rural life with the locals without losing the basic comforts of a hotel. Although many of the *casas de labranza* can be rented in their entirety there are very many in which you will be the 'guest' of the Spanish family which lives there. If you are interested in getting to know Spaniards as well as Spain then this is a splendid opportunity to get the flavour of family life.

If you rent an unoccupied house then you will naturally have the use of the facilities and the garden and you will cater for yourself. There are various ways of renting accommodation with a family – the most basic is just to rent a room on half board or full board – and there will be different rates depending how long you wish to stay; these rates will have to be negotiated with the owner. The Ministry of Tourism has a guide, called *Vacaciones en Casas de Labranza*, to all the houses in the scheme. This gives the owner's address and telephone number and lists all the facilities offered at each house. If you are sure that this is something you wish to try then you can write to the owner and make a booking. Although many are unlikely to be able to reply in English personally, they will most probably do so through the local tourist office.

If you are touring Spain and think that you might like to spend a night in such a place, then you can either use the guide to find the local owners, or go to the nearest tourist information office and ask the staff there to suggest suitable *casas* and make the necessary arrangements.

Useful
addresses

Spanish Camping Federation:

Federación Española de Campings
Gran Vía 88, Grupo 3 10° 8
Madrid 13
Tel: 1-242 3168

Camping and Caravan Club
11 Lower Grosvenor Place
London SW1
Tel: 01-828 10121

Camping and Outdoor Leisure Association
1 W. Ruislip Station

Ickenham Road
Ruislip
Tel: 0895-634191

For the *Casas de Labranza* guide:

Servicio de Información Turística
Secretaria General de Turismo
María de Molina 50
Madrid 28006
Tel: 91-411 40 14

Certain monasteries and convents offer accommo- **Monasteries**
dation for visitors in their *hospederías* (hospices or **and convents**
guest quarters). There is really only one which offers
hotel-like accommodation, including bathrooms, restaurant and bar, for individuals, couples or families
within the monastery. This is at the important
national shrine and centre of pilgrimage of the Virgin
of Guadalupe. Reservations can be made once there
or in advance at:

Hospedería del Real Monasterio
Plaza Juan Carlos 1 s/n
10140 Guadalupe
Cáceres
Tel: 927-36 70 00

There is a hotel associated with the other important
religious centre on the mountain of Montserrat near
Barcelona. Reservations can be made once there or
in advance at:

Hotel Abat Cisneros
Montserrat
Catalonia
Tel: 93-835 02 01

Alongside, and forming part of, the Benedictine
Monasterio de San Salvador de Leyre in Yesa,
Navarre, there are full, two-star hotel facilities at the
Hospedería de Leyre. The *hospedería* offers both
double and single rooms with complete bathrooms

and restaurant facilities. Once again, reservations can be made once there or in advance at:

Hospedería de Leyre
Monasterio de Leyre
Yesa 31410
Navarra
Tel: 948-88 41 00

A monastery in Mallorca offers *celdas* (literally 'cells') to tourists. These are available for two, four or six persons and have either WC and wash-basin or full bathroom facilities. Reservations should be made in advance through:

El Administrador
Monasterio del Santuario de Lluc
Mallorca
Tel: 71-51 70 96 or 71-51 70 25

Other monasteries and convents which offer accommodation for both men and women can be contacted at these addresses:

Padre Hospedero
Santuario Real de Montesclaros
Santander
Cantabria
Tel: 942-75 13 83

Here there are individual, two-bedded and three-bedded rooms with use of common toilets and showers. The food is homemade and an overnight stay will cost about 1400 pesetas.

Hermano Hospedero
Monasterio La Oliva
Carcastillo
Navarre
Tel: 948-72 50 06

The monastery was built in 1134 and is a fine example of Spanish Cistercian architecture. The monks announce that there is an atmosphere of seclusion and work here. A night's accommodation will cost between 500 and 1000 pesetas.

Other monasteries do offer accommodation, but in the course of research for this section the monks have asked that it be made clear that this is offered not simply to tourists but to those men who wish to share the spiritual life of the brothers for a few days. If you wish to make a retreat of this kind you must make a reservation prior to arrival and as far in advance as possible. The list below represents only those monasteries which have replied to a request for information.

Padre Hospedero
Abadia Cisterciense de San Pedro de Cardeña
Burgos
Tel: 947-29 00 33

The monks here are very willing to show tourists around this monastery, but again, only those who come for religious reasons may stay.

Hermano Santos García Vidal (Hospedero)
Abadia Cisterciense
Osera 32135
Orense
Tel: 988-28 20 04

The monastery has a *hospedería* with comfortable rooms for those who wish to go into retreat or to study, and the cost is approximately 1500 pesetas a day. The monastery suggests that it is best to visit after May because until that time it is rather cold there. Rooms can be reserved by post or by calling directly to Hermano Santos García, who can be most readily reached about 13.30, when he is in the refectory.

Hermano Hospedero
Monastir de Santa Maria de Poblet
Poblet 43448
Tarragona
Tel: 977-87 00 89

Here you will eat in the refectory with the Benedictine monks and follow their regime. There is no fixed price for staying, this is worked out according to your means.

Padre Hospedero
Abadia Cisterciense
Santa Maria de Huerta
Soria
Tel: 975-32 70 02

There are individual rooms available, which are simple but comfortable, and full board will cost 1000 pesetas a day.

Hermano Hospedero
Abadia Cisterciense de Nuestra Señora de San Isidro de Dueñas
Venta de Baños 34208
Palencia
Tel: 988-77 07 01

The monastery has a *hospedería*, and a modest fee is paid for full board by those in retreat.

Padre Hospedero
Abadia de Santo Domingo de Silos
Burgos
Tel: 947-38 07 68

Rooms in the *hospedería* have individual bathrooms with hot water and heating. A donation of about 1000 pesetas per day is requested for full board. This is a Benedictine establishment and you will be expected to observe the rules of silence and take part in the daily round of prayer. A stay in this monastery is especially interesting because it is an important centre for Gregorian plainsong.

It is more difficult to find accommodation which only allows women to stay. Most of the convents only take women who have arranged to stay through a church organization. The following, however, do accept female visitors:

Hermana Hospedera
Monasterio de la Inmaculada Concepción
Bajada del Barco 9
Toledo
Tel: 925-22 36 40

During academic terms this is a student residence
and it is always full at these times, but the nuns do
have rooms during the vacations.

Hermana Hospedera
Monasterio de Gradefes
Santa Maria la Real
Gradefes
León
Tel: 987-33 30 11

This is a Cistercian convent with very few rooms
and if you stay you will be expected to make a
donation for the food and accommodation.

Refúgios

These are over 200 mountain huts/houses established
to provide accommodation for hikers and mountain-
eers. Because they will only be of use to a very
particular group of tourists, information about them
is included in the 'Sport and leisure' chapter.

**Basic letter
for reserving
a hotel room**

Sr Administrador
Hotel Central
Plaza Mayor 10
Madrid
Spain

Estimado señor
Quisiera hacer una reserva de una habitación (dos
habitaciones) individual/doble (con cama individual/
dos camas individuales/con cama matrimonial) y con
baño/WC privado desde el [fecha] hasta [fecha].
Ruego que Vd tenga la bondad de confirmar la
reserva y comunicarme los precios lo más pronto
posible.
Le saludo muy atentamente

Sr Administrador
Hotel Central
Plaza Mayor
Madrid
Spain

Dear Sir
I would like to reserve a single/double room (two rooms) (with single bed/two single beds/double bed) and private bathroom/WC from [date] until [date]. Would you kindly confirm the reservation and send me the prices as soon as possible.
Yours sincerely

"This is the last time we come to Spain. You've spent the entire holiday worrying how they can afford to do it at the price."

Restaurants and bars

For Spaniards, drinking in bars and eating out are far more important as social occasions than as mere acts of consumption to satisfy either hunger or thirst, and bars are particularly important social centres. Eating out, whether it be taking a snack and a drink standing at a bar or actually sitting down to eat a complete meal in a restaurant, is a far more common event for a greater number of people and far less of a special occasion in Spain than it is in Britain, for example. You will also notice in restaurants (with the exception of those of the highest quality) that eating out is an important communal event in terms of families eating together, something which is possible because of the huge number of moderately priced establishments. Friends and families (and children very much form part of this) gather to eat, and although the enjoyment of food is important, even more so is the lively enjoyment of being together.

Restaurants are generally unpretentious and relaxed and the waiters non-intimidating. Most *camareros* (waiters or bar staff) work with great style whether they are cleaning the bar counter (something they seem to be addicted to) or serving a dozen demanding customers at the same time. Although somewhat exaggeratedly, the great Hispanophile Gerald Brennan captured the sense of this when he commented

> they have the air of bullfighters *manqués*, of *toreros* who wisely prefer the white napkin to the red cloth and the pacific diner to the charging bull. They move with the same litheness and ballet dancer's precision and put a certain solemn operatic air into every gesture. How refreshing to see people doing the supposedly humdrum and mechanical things with artistic relish and gusto! (*The Face of Spain* [Penguin 1987], 21)

If you wish to hear a fine piece of Spanish popular recitation try asking a waiter in a bar which has a wide range of *tapas* (snacks) '*¿Que hay de tapas?*' ('What sorts of *tapas* are there?'). The result is likely to be a rendition, at machine-gun speed, of the entire list. Some seem to favour short-burst deliveries of sections of the list, perhaps in the hope that they will not have to cover everything. The waiters who go for the continuous quick-fire approach seem to take a deep breath as they begin the word '*Hay*. . . '('There are. . . '); the *hay* is drawn out, there is a moment's pause and they are off – usually starting with *albondigas* (meat balls) and ending with something involving *zanahorias* (carrots). The only trouble is that you will probably be lost after the first couple of items, but don't worry; most Spaniards have assured me, when asked whether they can follow everything, that all they do is to listen out for things which might interest them.

Bars Spanish bars are not simply drinking establishments serving alcohol. Should you wish to do so you would be able to find bars to satisfy all your food and drink requirements from breakfast to dinner, as well as for the sociable drinking which takes place around midday and in the evening.

Coffee The majority of bars, except for some older establishments which mainly serve wines, will have an *espresso*-style coffee machine and offer coffee prepared in a variety of ways. Fortunately instant coffee or the thin, almost flavourless liquid which passes for 'freshly brewed' or 'real' coffee in many countries is virtually unknown in Spanish bars, and the advertisers have yet to persuade the public that really satisfying coffee is something 'mild' or 'mellow' which has the aroma of gravy browning.

The simplest preparation is *café solo* (black *espresso* coffee), which is served as a small cup or glass of dark, pungent coffee. *Café con leche* (coffee with milk) is white coffee, made with the same amount of coffee as a *café solo* plus hot milk; *café cortado* is white coffee but with very little milk; and *leche manchada* is exactly the opposite, being literally 'stained milk' – a cup or glass of hot milk with very little coffee added. In the summer *café con hielo* (iced coffee), a long black coffee with ice-cubes, is refreshing. Decaffeinated coffee, *descafeinado*, is served in most bars and is usually a sachet of Nescafé decaffeinated powder added to a glass of hot milk.

One form of preparing coffee deserves special mention; this is the *carajillo*. At its most basic it is a measure of brandy added to a *café solo*; but if the waiter knows how or has the time to make it properly he will place a little sugar and the brandy into a glass and, using the steam pipe of the *espresso* machine, warm the liquid. This will then be set on fire and after a few moments the *café solo* will be added to it. The resulting *carajillo* will usually be served with a small slice of lemon and a coffee bean floating on top. A carajillo can also be made with anís (an aniseed liquor).

Tea

Té in a Spanish bar is made with hot water from the *espresso* machine to which is added a tea-bag and usually a slice of lemon. If you want tea with milk you have a bit of a problem, because it is not usually drunk this way. A request for *té con leche* will get you a fairly disagreeable mixture of hot milk with a tea-bag, so it is best to try asking for a *té con un poquito de leche fria* (tea with a little cold milk).

A very popular soothing infusion is that of camomile tea (*manzanilla*). There can be confusion over this, though, because it has the same name as one of the *fino* wines (see 'Wine and other drinks'), so if the barman heads for a bottle tell him that it is a *té de manzanilla* that you want.

Alcoholic drinks

Spanish bars do not operate licensing hours and so you can be served alcoholic drinks from the moment the bar is open in the morning until the time the owner decides to close. The chapter on 'Wine and other drinks' gives information about the sorts of drink available, but it is worth mentioning how to order them.

Beer (*cerveza*) comes either in bottles or, more usually, from the barrel and different regions seem to have different names for the measures, so it is simplest to ask for *una cerveza* (a beer). Beer is rarely served in anything as large as a glass resembling a British pint, although if it is it is called *una jarra*; but this can be confusing because a *jarra* can also be a jug or a pitcher, and beer is sometimes also served this way if there is a group drinking. More commonly beer is served in a small glass called *una caña* or in a slightly larger one known as *un tanque* or *un tubo*.

For wine (*vino*) you need only ask for *un tinto* (red wine) or *un blanco* (a white wine), and if you want a bottle ask for *una botella de . . .* (a bottle of. . .) and then specify the colour or brand you require. Sherry wines should be served in a special glass called a *copita*, so you can either ask for *una copita de. . .* or simply name the type of sherry. For spirits and liqueurs (see 'Wine and other drinks') you only need to ask for the type you require.

Soft drinks   Generically known as *refrescos*, there is a variety to choose from, and they are simply ordered by their brand names. It is a rare bar which does not stock the ubiquitous Coca Cola, but there is also *Tab* which is like Coca Cola but without caffeine or calories, Fanta either *de limón* (lemon) or *de naranja* (orange), the Schweppes range and Bitter Kas. *Agua mineral* (mineral water) is available either *con gas* (with carbonation) or *sin gas* (without). Ice is *hielo*. Most bars have a refrigerated tap for cold water and it is perfectly acceptable to ask for *un vaso de agua fría* (a glass of cold water). This is often automatically served if you ask for a coffee.

Fruit juices   Despite the enormous fruit production it is surprisingly difficult to get good fruit juice in Spain, and Spaniards rarely seem to ask for it. A request for *un zumo* or *un jugo* (a juice) is likely to get you a highly sweetened juice, and if you want fresh juice you should ask for a *zumo natural*. The most likely place to find it is in the more modern bars.

In an uncrowded bar you will obviously have no difficulty in being served, but if it is busy and you shyly wait to be served you may wait for a considerable time. Spaniards in this situation tend just to shout their requests in the general direction of the waiters, and somewhat surprisingly this results in their drinks being brought to them, even though the waiter might not have outwardly registered that he had heard and might have even had his back to them at the time. The best way for visitors to get a waiter's attention is to call *'¡Oiga, por favor!'* ('Listen please' or 'Attention please') and then make their request.

As in many parts of Europe, the price you pay for a drink may depend on where in the bar you consume it. If the bar has seating and waiter service there will be one price for consuming your drink at the counter, another if you are seated within the bar and yet another if you sit outside. It is not acceptable to pay for your drink at the counter and then to take it outside if there is such waiter service. In the majority of bars you will be expected to pay only when you have finished your consumption. The exception to this is in some bars where you are able to sit at tables on the pavement, where the waiters may well ask for payment when they have served you. This is especially the case in some tourist centres, where unfortunately some customers have slipped away without paying and therefore a sense of mistrust has crept in.

Either a running total is chalked on the counter itself or a note is kept under it, and because of this it is somewhat difficult to drink and pay in terms of the traditional, and calculated, British 'round'. Spaniards do not generally drink in this way and if a group of friends are drinking in a bar one of them will pay the bill when they have finished. The social pattern of who is 'invited' to drink by whom is complex, and you will often see Spaniards arguing over who is to be allowed to pay the whole bill.

They will take out money and try to force it on the waiter while others will push their money forward, physically restrain their friends, and insist that *theirs* be accepted. Waiters seem skilled in deciding from whom they ought to accept the money when there are several offering it.

On the other hand, especially in places away from the tourist areas, waiters are therefore often bemused by or disdainful of foreigners who try to work out what each has drunk and to pay separate parts of the bill (which because of the comparatively low cost of drinks is usually not very great). It is rare that Spaniards will stay in one bar all night and so during the course of the evening each will have the chance to insist on the right to 'invite' his friends, but this is certainly not a conscious attempt to equalize the payments.

Although it is not expected that you will leave a certain percentage as a tip after drinks in a bar, it is good manners to leave a small amount of your change.

Bar facilities   A service which most bars provide is that of *servicios* (lavatories/toilets). Public lavatories tend to be scarce in Spain so bars are particularly important. Even if you are not drinking or eating in a bar the owners or waiters do not generally seem to object to members of the public using the lavatories. Simply ask '¿*Donde estan los servicios?*' ('Where are the lavatories?') or '¿*Hay servicios?*' ('Are there any lavatories?'). You should then look for the doors marked *caballeros* (gentlemen) and *señoras* (ladies). In some older bars you will find evidence of the fact that bars were once all-male preserves – there may only be a stand-up urinal.

You should be warned that most bar lavatories are not particularly salubrious places and many visitors are put off by the commonly encountered device where you have to squat over a hole with your feet placed on two raised sections within a low enamel basin. Some people claim that these are both uncomfortable and insanitary. With regard to the first point, it is fairly easy to accustom yourself to this position, and with regard to the second, I would suggest that it is infinitely preferable to have the private parts of your anatomy in mid air than in contact with certain of the toilet bowls you are likely to encounter. Many bars and public lavatories do not supply lavatory paper and it is advisable to take something with you.

A warning: because of the poor quality of much of the Spanish sewerage system, it is common practice to leave used lavatory paper in the wastepaper basket found in the corner of most stalls (or even on the floor). This is likely to be extremely disagreeable to many visitors, but as this necessary habit is widespread it is best to be prepared.

In this chapter a good deal of attention has been given to bars because Spaniards consume so much standing at bar counters, and because it is this which is likely to strike the tourist more than the fairly obvious event of sitting at a table in a restaurant and eating a complete meal. Naturally there are, in most towns, a wide range of restaurants to choose from, from those specializing in first class Spanish and international cuisine, through those with regional specialities, to the humbler family establishments. Alongside the highways you will also see *ventas*, which are establishments which usually combine bars and restaurants. Those restaurants at the highest quality and price level will be found listed in the Michelin Red Book, but because of the popularity of eating in restaurants you are likely to eat well and cheaply in the ones catering for the more popular demand.

Bars and restaurants

Tapas are small bar snacks which are consumed with drinks and are usually available both at midday and in the evening. Originally bars would offer a slice of ham, cheese, a piece of fish or a simple vegetable dish free to those buying a glass of wine, but nowadays the variety is far greater and they must be paid for, although some bars will give you a few olives with a drink. (Incidentally, if you wish to be particularly Spanish do not eat the last olive; this is

Tapas

called *la vergüenza* – literally 'the shame' – and should be left in the bowl.)

Although *tapas* can be found all over Spain the custom of eating *de tapas* is perhaps most developed in the south, where bars can be found which offer dozens of items on their *tapa* list. For those who do not wish to sit down to a main meal and who wish to experience a variety of dishes, then, this is an ideal and cheap way to eat. A particularly delightful way to savour the local tastes and wines is to do as the Spaniards do and stroll from bar to bar having a couple of *tapas* and a glass of wine in each of them. Should you find something which you particularly like and of which you would like a more substantial quantity, ask the waiter to give you *una ración* (a portion).

Most bars which serve *tapas* will also make sandwiches for you. These are usually of cheese, ham, *chorizo* (the spiced sausage) or *tortilla* (omelette, particularly the Spanish speciality *tortilla de patatas* – potato omelette), but might include other items from the *tapa* list. Although the word *sandwich* has gained currency in many parts of Spain, it is only used for the thin sandwiches, often toasted, made of processed bread. The native sandwiching of a filling in a substantial bread roll is far more satisfying and is called a *bocadillo*.

Meals

Breakfast

Desayuno (breakfast) is likely to be served until about 11.00 because many working Spaniards leave their houses early, having had little more than a coffee, and then leave their office after a couple of hours to have breakfast. Unless you are staying in a hotel, you should note that you are unlikely to find more than a few simple pastries and toast on offer in most bars. As with *bocadillos*, *tostada* (toast) is usually a large toasted roll, although some more 'sophisticated' bars will toast processed bread.

There are two important items which Spaniards put on their toast, *mantaquilla* (butter, although unless it comes in small individual packs it is quite often actually margarine) and *aceite* (olive oil). Although it might seem strange to use olive oil it really is worth trying it at least once, and should you really wish to imitate the locals you can go one better and rub your toast with the garlic clove which is supplied before you pour on the oil. In addition to the coffee and toast, breakfast in a bar for many Spaniards also means a shot of alcohol, and you will see many having a glass of brandy, *anís* or *aguardiente*.

Despite the country's enormous fruit production and the fact that Seville has given its name to marmalade oranges, Spaniards don't eat marmalade. If you want something sweet on your toast ask for *mermelada*, which is actually jam and will come in small plastic packets. Your toast will not usually come pre-spread and the waiter will ask you what you want to put on it – the tubs of butter/margarine and bottles of olive oil will be clearly visible on the bar and all you need to do is to indicate what you want. In most bars at breakfast time you will also see bowls of gaudy coloured pastes on offer. These are various kinds of pig fat (the generic name of which is *manteca*) with other meat additives, and these are also typical breakfast spreads. Different regions have different styles and names, but the most common are *manteca amarilla*, which is a basic white/yellow lard, *manteca colorada*, which is orange-coloured and has paprika or cayenne added, *sobra-sada*, which has pieces of chorizo in it, and *chich-arones*, which is white and has chopped meat added.

If such strong tastes do not appeal first thing in the morning and you want something sweeter, some bars will serve *croisantes*, the nearest Spanish equivalent to French croissants but tending to be sweeter and heavier. *Madelenas* (small sponge cakes) are common breakfast fare, and bars which have these are likely to have a range of other sponge-like confections on display. *Torrija*, a rich breakfast food found in some parts of the country, consists of bread which has been soaked in either wine, milk or water, and is then fried and covered in honey.

Finally there is a national 'dish' which really ought to be tried – *churros*. *Churros* have a slight resemblance to certain styles of doughnut and are made from a flour and water paste which is forced through a nozzle into a huge bowl of boiling oil. As the mixture begins to hit the oil the *churrero* (the *churro* maker) uses two long sticks to spin it into a large spiral. It is cooked for a few moments, lifted out and drained (well, almost drained) of excess oil, cut into strips and weighed out for each customer. Although bars rarely make *churros* themselves it is perfectly acceptable to buy them at the stall and then take them to the bar, to be eaten with a breakfast coffee; you will see plenty of people clutching greasy bundles at the counter if there is a stall nearby.

How to find a *churro*? You can either ask '*¿Hay un puesto de churros por aquí?*' ('Is there a *churro* stall around here?') or just follow your nose – the smell is both distinctive and pervasive, and clouds of smoke billowing out of a doorway or window also indicate that you are on the right track. Some *churro* stalls will serve cups of hot, thick chocolate, and *churros y chocolate* is a favourite with Spaniards late at night or early in the morning as they go home after celebrating at the *feria* (the local fair).

You should be warned, however, that *churros* do tend to sit heavily on the stomach. As James Michener, in his book *Iberia* (Random House 1968), comments after reluctantly succumbing to the temptation, 'Churros and chocolate! I suppose if one searched the restaurants of the world one could not find a worse breakfast nor one that tasted better. . . Any nation that can eat *churros* and chocolate for breakfast is not required to demonstrate its courage in other ways.'

Lunch   *Almuerzo* (lunch) in many parts of Spain is referred to as *la comida* (literally 'the food'), a term which emphasizes the importance of this for many people as the central meal. It is usually taken between about 14.00 and 16.00, and you will certainly find bars and restaurants busy at this time. If you do not want to go to a restaurant it will not take you long to find a bar with a few tables that is serving lunch, probably mainly to working men, and although the range of foods on offer might not be great you should be able to eat well and the portions will be substantial.

It is also worth noting that most restaurants will offer a *menú del dia* (menu of the day), which is a set-price meal of three courses with bread and a glass of wine or beer included. Even though this has a set price you are very likely to find two or three things to choose between for each course. If you want to see the full menu ask for *el menú* (although in some parts of Spain *el menú* means the set-price meals) or *la carta*, and when you have finished your meal you will need to ask for *la cuenta por favor* (the bill, please).

A service charge is not usually included; if it is you will see the words *servicio incluido*. The top amount for a tip in the more expensive restaurants is about 10 per cent, but this would be fairly high for the more modest ones, where it would be perfectly acceptable to leave a small amount of change. In such small restaurants, even where the service charge might be included, it is considered good manners to leave some change.

Cena (dinner) is eaten usually at the very earliest at 20.00 but more commonly from about 21.00 until maybe 23.00, although in the winter it is usually somewhat earlier. In fact in many towns it is often rather difficult to find anything substantial to eat between about 17.00 and 19.30. Many of the bars which offer a sit-down lunch will not provide the same service at night, when they concentrate more on serving drinks, but you will not have any difficulty in finding places to eat for a modest cost.

Dinner

Restaurants in Spain do not generally have no-smoking sections. Smoking is a very common Spanish practice and you are likely to find diners smoking not only before and after their meals but also between courses. The only advice which can be offered here is that if smoke particularly troubles you, try to get near a window. If you are visiting in the summer when windows are likely to be open you should not have to suffer too much.

Smoking

It is worth making a separate point about smoking. If you are a smoker and come from a culture where each person smokes their own cigarettes or waits to be offered one by another smoker, you will find things very different in Spain. Cigarettes are very cheap and in a large group of Spaniards there are likely to be more smokers (both men and women) than non-smokers; you will be readily offered cigarettes, so it is advisable to have some with you to share. If you do not have any but want to smoke you are unlikely to be regarded as a scrounger, for the Spanish sense of sociable hospitality means that the counting of who has had what is ungracious. When socializing with a group of people whom you have got to know it is perfectly acceptable to take a cigarette from one of the packets which will inevitably be on the table or bar, although it is polite to ask '¿*Puedo*. . . ?' ('May I?') the first time.

For different types of cigarette and where to buy them see 'Shopping'.

Foreign and fast foods   The range and quality of Spanish cuisine is so good that it is difficult to imagine that someone would not be able to find food to suit their taste, but should you want non-Spanish food then you will have to look in the tourist areas and the big cities. In the tourist areas (especially on the Mediterranean coasts) you will find restaurants serving English, German and American styles of food, and in the main cities such as Madrid or Barcelona you will find many restaurants serving the cuisine of other parts of the world. In recent years basic Chinese restaurants have been established even in some smaller cities, although they do not seem to be particularly popular.

Fast food (usually only found in large cities) is not something which forms an important part of Spaniards' eating patterns, and with the range of *tapas*, other Spanish snacks and moderately priced restaurants available to them this is hardly surprising. The variety of fast food that can be found is not great, although *hamburgesas* (hamburgers – establishments such as McDonalds and Burger King have entered the Spanish market) and *pizzerias* can be found.

Food

In the context of a non-specialist guide of this type it is difficult to do more than point to some of the main types of cuisine and wine which are to be found in Spain so that you can look out for them in restaurants. Once again it is worth recommending certain guides which either are worth taking with you or you can refer to at home.

Specialist guides

Obviously you do not want to be weighed down with an entire library but there is a slim, easily portable book, *Spanish Wines* (1988) by Jan Read (one of the Mitchell Beazley Pocket Guides to wines), which is invaluable for travellers who are interested in food and wine. Jan Read is a recognized authority on Spanish wines and this guide describes all twelve wine regions, gives information about the different styles of wine, spirits and liqueurs, and most usefully rates the quality of the wines according to year. At the end of each regional section Read also gives a short account of the specialities of the regional cuisine. The quality and quantity of information which he packs into 150 small pages makes it an essential item for the traveller who wishes to be guided towards drinking and eating well.

Two other recently published books must be recommended for those who would like more detailed information about these subjects. In *The Wine and Food of Spain* (Weidenfeld and Nicolson 1987) Jan Read, with his wife Maite Manjón (a cookery writer) and the internationally renowned wine writer Hugh Johnson, have produced a well-illustrated and extremely informative region-by-region guide. The second recent book is *The Spanish Table* (Ebury Press 1987), written by Marimar Torres, who is a member of the famous Torres wine family. As one of the reviewers of the book has written, 'I can't imagine ever needing another book of Spanish food and wine.' Not only does this contain a detailed analysis of all Spanish cuisine and a range of the finest recipes, but it also gives information about the wines and the wine producers (with telephone numbers should you wish to arrange a visit), and an appendix of the best restaurants of Spain and their specialities. Both of these books, though, are for reading at home, whereas *Spanish Wines* is designed for carrying in your pocket.

As was mentioned above it is impossible in this sort of guide to do justice to the variety of Spanish cuisine, and what follows should not be regarded as more than a thumbnail sketch of some of the main types of dish. The regions mentioned below do not correspond to geographical or cultural regions, but rather certain provinces have been grouped as gastronomic regions.

Andalusia Andalusia is often referred to by cookery writers as the region of fried food (especially because of the quantity and quality of the olive oil locally available), but this should not be taken to imply that it is greasy food. Fish, for example, in the mixed fish dishes known as *pescaíto frito*, are deep fried but are dry on the outside and moist inisde. High quality fish and shellfish can be found, particularly on the Atlantic coast, and freshly grilled sardines (*sardinas*) should definitely be tried. A well-known Andalusian summer dish is the cold *gazpacho* soup, which is based on bread, oil, garlic, water, tomatoes and other salad vegetables. In Malaga there is a milky-white varient of *gazpacho* which is made of almonds, oil and garlic.

Although *tapas* (the hors d'oeuvre-like little bar snacks) are found in most parts of Spain, they form a particularly important part of the eating habits in Andalusia. The bars of Seville probably produce the finest range, with some offering up to thirty or forty at any one time.

The Moorish influence is particularly noticeable in the desserts, for the majority of Spanish pastries are based on almonds. Desserts made with egg yolks as a main ingredient are common throughout Spain, and Marimar Torres suggests that the importance given to egg yolks originates from Jerez, where egg whites were used to clarify sherries. The egg yolks were traditionally given to convents, with the result that nuns became justly famous for their custards and egg caramel dishes. Today *natillas* (custard) or *flan* (egg custard) are very popular desserts and in restaurants you should look out for *flan de la casa*, which will be homemade.

A word of advice: in many towns and cities in Andalusia you will see orange trees growing along the streets. These are attractive and give a wonderful scent in the spring, but do not attempt to eat the oranges – they are the sort used to make marmalade and are extremely bitter.

Extremadura

This region is held in high regard for the quality of its *embutidos* or *chacinas* (hams and sausages). This comes about because of the combination of a dry climate, mountains, the extensive oak forests and the black *cerdo iberico* (a native pig which is closely related to the wild boar), which lives on the acorns. It is the meat from this pig which is used to make the best *jamón serrano* (mountain ham), legs of which you will find hanging in many bars.

These hams take between eighteen months and three years to cure. They are first rubbed with salt for about two weeks and then hung in drying rooms, where the dry mountain air works its effect. The ham from the *cerdo iberico* is known as *pata negra* (literally 'black leg') because of its dark colour and its easily identifiable black hoof, which is always left on the joint. Other varieties of pig which are used for *jamón serrano* are stall-fed and the ham, although fine, does not have quite the same quality. The single most famous Spanish village for its hams is Jabugo, which is actually just outside of Extremadura in northern Andalusia, and Jabugo hams can be found hanging in bars in many parts of Spain.

From other parts of the slaughtered pig come the spicy sausages such as *chorizo, caña de lomo, morcon, salchicha* and the blood sausage *morcilla*, all of which will be seen hanging in bars and restaurants not only in Extremadura but all over Spain. Many of these pork specialities find their way into an old Extremaduran dish called *cachuela*, which is a dark, rich meat stew consisting of *chorizo, morcilla*, off-cuts of pork and lamb, pieces of heart, liver and kidneys, and almonds. This dish is so heavy that it is rarely eaten as a complete meal and is usually served as a *tapa* (bar snack)

A very special meat which can sometimes be found is *jabalí* (wild boar). These animals are hunted in many parts of Extremadura but the availability of the meat very much depends on the luck of the hunters.

Castile–La Mancha   This area, which covers several provinces, is referred to as the region of the roast meats, with lamb, sucking pig and kid being the most interesting of them. In the area between Segovia, Soria and Burgos, roast lamb is a particular delicacy. Look out for the word *lechazo* on menus; this is a roasted baby lamb which has been fed only on its mother's milk. Another speciality of the region is *chueltas de cordero* (lamb chops) – you will see from the tiny bones how young the animals were when slaughtered. The other important culinary triangle is that of Segovia–Arévalo–Peñaranda, within which you will find the best *cochinillo* or *tostón* (roast sucking pig). Again the unweaned babies are slaughtered extremely young, normally between 15 and 20 days, and the meat when roasted is so tender that it is said that it can be cut with the side of a plate – and in some restaurants it is.

A famous Madrid dish is the *cocido madrileño* or *cocido castellano*, which is a substantial stew made from chick peas, chunks of beef, bacon, spicy sausage, blood pudding, potatoes, turnips and cabbage or spinach. As can be imagined from the list of ingredients this is often served as a meal in itself, with the strained broth forming the first part, the vegetables the second, and the cut-up meats as a final part.

A classic dish from La Mancha which can be found in many parts of Spain is *pisto manchego*, which is a vegetable dish somewhat like ratatouille. In its classic form it is only made with red and green peppers, tomatoes and courgettes, but it is nowadays found with many other vegetable ingredients and often ham or bacon.

La Mancha produces Spain's most well-known cheese, the sheep's milk cheese *Manchego*. This is sometimes soaked in olive oil for anything between a few weeks and over a year. You may find it in some bars; if you enjoy piquant cheese do try it with a glass of *fino* sherry.

The sweet to look out for is *marzapán* (marzipan). Although one legend has it that it was invented in the thirteenth century in a convent in Toledo (certainly the professional guides of Toledo tell the story), marzipan is an Arabic confection. The modern art of its manufacture has been raised to a level of excellence in Toledo and you will find many shops selling it there.

The Levante

The Levante is that part of the Mediterranean coastland which extends from approximately Alicante to just south of Tarragona. The coastal strip is extremely fertile and is a huge market garden area, producing wonderful fruit (particularly oranges) and vegetables. The market in Valencia, which offers a wide range of these, is well worth a visit.

This area is the main rice-producing zone of Spain and, quite naturally, rice dishes are a speciality within the cuisine. *Paella* is internationally known and is regarded by many as almost the national dish of Spain. There seem to be as many recipes for *paella* as there are Spaniards who have an opinion on it. Some writers suggest that the 'original' *paella* contained only eels, snails (both of which are regional specialities), peas and saffron-flavoured rice, but the *paella valenciana* or classic modern *paella* has shellfish, chicken and pork as its main ingredients. If you are going to eat *paella* it is best to treat it as a special meal in itself rather than as part of a meal, or you are likely to be served a quickly thrown together and somewhat stodgy mixture. If you are interested in making the dish at home it is well worth going to a supermarket or an ironmongers and buying a proper *paellera* (a round, shallow iron or aluminium pan); they are very cheap and come in a great variety of dimensions.

Catalonia   Most commentators on Spain would probably agree that Catalan (along with Basque) cuisine is the most sophisticated of Spain, and for those who enjoy fine food the restaurants of Barcelona (Marimar Torres tells us that there are over 10,000 eating establishments in the city) will soon dispel any prejudice that Spanish cuisine has little more to offer than well-prepared rural fare, or is dull and uniform. Catalonia is often referred to as the 'zone of the sauces'. There are five main types: *ali-oli*, which is an emulsion formed by pounding garlic and olive oil with a pestle and mortar; *picada*, which is again a pounded mixture, this time of garlic, parsley, almonds and hazelnuts; *samfaina*, which is a mixture of peppers, tomatoes, aubergine, onion and garlic sautéed in oil; *romesco*, a paste of toasted almonds, dried red peppers, garlic, tomatoes and bread; and *sofrito*, a sautéed mixture of finely chopped tomatoes, onions, peppers and parsley. These different sauces are then used to accompany a variety of meats and fish.

A bread dish which really ought to be tried is *pan con tomate* (bread with tomato), which consists of thick slices of heavy bread rubbed with tomato, garlic and salt. It is sometimes served with ham.

In Barcelona people seem particularly addicted to the fine range of pastries available, and if you want to try an especially filling dessert ask for a *pijama* (literally 'pyjamas') – an egg custard surrounded by whipped cream and often topped with ice cream for good measure.

Navarre   The mountain streams of Navarre are famous for their trout (*truchas*), which in restaurants are usually served stuffed with ham. Game birds such as *cordoniz* (quail), *perdiz* (partridge), *torcaz* (wood pigeon sometimes called *pichón* when it appears on a menu) are specialities, but their availability does vary according to what has been shot.

Pamplona, the provincial capital, is famous for its *chorizos* and other spiced sausages such as *chistorra*. Unlike the style of sausages made in Extremadura, which are not cooked at all, the majority of these have been boiled.

A particularly fine cheese comes from Navarre. This is a raw sheep's milk cheese called *Roncal*, which is made in the Pyrenean valley of the same name.

Aragon

The most notable item of Aragonese cuisine (although it is also found in Navarre) is *chilindrón* sauce. This is a sautéed mixture of tomatoes, onions and bell peppers, but its most noticeable feature is dried chilli peppers. The sauce, which can often be quite hot, is used in the preparation of chicken, pork and lamb. Once again lambs in this region are slaughtered young and the roasted meat is delicious. Hams (*jamón serrano*) cured in the mountain villages to the east and west of Teruel are particularly fine.

Asturias

The dish which Asturias has given to Spanish cuisine is a thick stew called *fabada*, which takes its name from the *fabes* (large white beans) which are an essential ingredient. In a *fabada* these are cooked with a variety of pork products including bacon, black pudding, *chorizo* and another sausage called *longaniza*.

Although *arroz con leche* (rice pudding) can be found all over Spain the particularly high quality of Asturian milk makes this dish special in the region. It should be mentioned, though, that in general milk in Spain, being variously processed for long life, is fairly horrible.

Asturias also produces a range of cheeses, the most famous of which is *Cabrales-Picón*. *Picón* is a very strong blue-veined cheese, formed by mixing cow's, sheep's and goat's milk, which is wrapped in chestnut leaves to mature; and *Cabrales* refers to the village where the best of it is made.

Galicia

If you want to indulge in seafood then go to Galicia, but do have a small dictionary or phrase book with you to identify the enormous variety of fish and tentacled and shelled beasties. If there are speciality dishes which ought to be picked out they are *vieiras*, which are scallops in their shells baked with a simple mixture of pepper, onions, parsley and bread crumbs, and *pulpo a feira*, which is octopus prepared with oil, salt and paprika. *Empanadas* (pies or tarts) are also a Galician speciality. They are savoury and filled with various meats or fish; those filled with freshly grilled *sardinas* (sardines) are particularly flavoursome.

Almond-based cakes and biscuits are favourite desserts.

The Basque country

Basque cuisine ranks with that of Catalonia and the people here are famous in Spain for their passion for and knowledge of food. This concern for food is given an institutional form in the 1000 or so gastronomic societies which exist in the region, and also in the development of a totally Basque version of nouvelle cuisine.

Although traditional Basque cuisine is extremely varied, the seafood dishes are perhaps the most famous. One of the oldest is *Marmitako*, a rich, fishermen's stew made of tuna and other fish mixed with tomatoes and potatoes. *Angulas* (baby eels which are usually no bigger than a matchstick) is a dish which can sometimes be found in other parts

"Oh, forget it – we'll have the steak!"

of Spain but, because of the quality of the eels themselves, should be tried here. They are usually served as *angulas al ajillo* and appear in small earthenware bowls with sizzling hot oil, garlic and chilli peppers. Marimar Torres suggests that the Basque *calamares en su tinta* (squid in their ink) is the only true black dish in the world, and that this can be made because Basque fishermen catch the squid on hooks and lines so that they do not exude most of their ink as they do when they are caught in nets.

Those who normally eat their cod fried should try *bacalao a la vizcaína* (salt cod in the Vizcaya style), which is salt cod prepared in a sauce of red peppers, onions, garlic and breadcrumbs. Cod in Spain, because it is salt-dried when it is bought from the shops, has a much stronger taste than fresh cod.

Balearics

As might be expected from a Mediterranean group of islands, seafood is an important speciality. Notable dishes ae *calamares a la mallorquina* (squid in the Mallorcan style), in which the squid is stuffed with pine kernels and raisins, and *caldereta de datiles*, which is soup made from a 'sea date' (a small brown mussel).

Of the meats pork is the best treated, especially as charcuterie, and perhaps the most famous product is *sobrasada*, which is a paprika-coloured pork spread for use on bread or for flavouring stews. *El tumbet* is an interesting vegetable dish made of layers of potatoes and fried aubergine, which is then covered with a tomato and pepper sauce.

In Mallorca particular breakfast specialities are the cakes called *ensaimadas*. Once again these depend on pork products, for they are made with lard.

Canaries

Perhaps the single most famous dish from these islands is *papas arrugadas* (literally 'wrinkled potatoes'). For this dish the unpeeled potatoes are boiled in sea water (although often today ordinary water, heavily salted, is used) and then baked. These potatoes are usually served with *mojo colorado* or *mojo picón*, a spicy sauce containing garlic, olive oil, cayenne, chilli pepper and cumin seeds. This sauce is also used for various fish and meat dishes, one of which is *sancorcho*, a fish stew. It is usually based on dried and salted fish, of which *cherna* (grouper) or *sama* (porgy, which is a type of sea bream) are the usual varieties. These are soaked in water to remove some of the saltiness before cooking. A complete dish would be *sancorcho* with *papas arrugadas*, sweet potatoes and *mojo*.

Another important item of the cuisine is *gofio*, which is toasted and ground millet mixed with water, oil, salt and sugar, formed into a ball and baked. It is then eaten as a form of bread.

Some unusual tastes

Apart from the major regional specialities, you might like to try somewhat more unusual bits and pieces of animals which can be found in bars and restaurants in many parts of the country:

Pestorejo – pig's ear prepared in oil and vinegar

Sangre – blood cooked with onions (often advertised as *sangre encebollada*)

Criadillas – testicles (usually pig's testicles) in sauce

Menudo – giblets or other small parts of offal in a slightly spicy sauce

Callos – tripe, somewhat similar to *menudo*, and quite often served as *callos al ajo* (tripe with garlic)

Mollejas – in some parts of Spain, particularly Extremadura, this is chickens' gizzards prepared in sauce, and in others it is lightly fried pancreas (sweetbreads)

Pajaritos – roasted songbirds. This dish is now illegal but it can sometimes be found in bars in areas where birds are trapped in the countryside. The birds are served whole (with legs and heads but de-beaked), and some may find the idea repellent, but the birds do have a most delicate taste.

Wine and other drinks

As was the case with the introduction to regional cuisine above, this section can be little more than a thumbnail sketch of Spanish wines and other drinks. Once again, it is highly recommended that the traveller who has a discerning palate and an interest in wine should carry Jan Read's guide, *Spanish Wines* (Mitchell Beazley 1988). In general Spaniards are neither pretentious nor elitist about their wines and wine drinking; for most it is simply a pleasant (and necessary) accompaniment to a meal. As Jan Read et al. have written in *The Wine and Food of Spain* (Weidenfeld and Nicolson 1987), 'In much of Spain. . . wine is still regarded as a commodity of scarcely more interest than bread.' With an annual average consumption of some 70 litres per person, wine obviously forms an essential part of Spanish life both at home with meals and in bars and restaurants. *Vino* (wine) is either *tinto* (red) or *blanco* (white), although rosés (*rosados*) can also be found, and over the bar you would simply ask for either *un tinto* or *un blanco*. Do not be surprised if in bars and the more modest restaurants (particularly in the south) the red comes chilled, since this is regarded as a refreshing drink in the summer.

There are twenty-six officially demarcated wine-producing areas, controlled by legislation from a department of the Ministry of Agriculture and, as is done by Marimar Torres in her survey, these can be very roughly divided into three main zones. The southern zone (basically Andalusia) produces aperitif wines, which tend to be known as sherries in English, and the dessert wines of Montilla-Mories and Malaga. The central zone produces the greatest bulk of wine in the form of less delicate table wines, the most well-known denomination being Valdepeñas. The northern belt comprises Galicia, the Upper Duero, Rioja and Catalonia, and produces the best red and white wines.

The southern zone

The sherries

For many people the image of sherry is that of the sweet, brown liquid reputedly beloved of vicars and acceptable for grandmother at Christmas lunch, but in Andalusia the sherry wines are very different. The wines produced in the areas around Jerez de la Frontera (from which the name *jerez* or sherry derives), Puerto de Santa Maria, Cadiz and Sanlucar de Barrameda are mainly light, dry aperitif wines. Although there are a number of varieties the *finos* are the palest and driest. They are served chilled in a *copita*, a narrow glass which tapers inwards towards the top, and are ideal as a midday drink with *tapas* (bar snacks). Because *finos* deteriorate if left for too long in the bottle, half bottles are produced, and in a bar you can ask for *una media botella de fino* (a half bottle of *fino*); although in many bars in this region the *finos* will be served directly from barrels and you can then enjoy trying the range on display.

A wonderful variety is *manzanilla*, produced in Sanlucar de Barrameda at the mouth of the Guadalquivir river. Although this can be found in many places in Andalusia (and generally throughout Spain) connoisseurs claim that its slightly salty tang can only be fully appreciated if drunk in Sanlucar itself. Two other important varieties are *amontillado*, which is dry and amber-coloured but somewhat smoother than the *fino*, and *oloroso*, which is dark and very full-bodied. It should be noted that there are both dry and semi-sweet varieties of *oloroso*, and if you want the dry variety you should ask for *oloroso seco*.

If you are in Jerez it is well worth while making a tour of the *bodegas* (wineries). The large ones (although there are others), such as Gonzalez Byass, which makes the famous *fino Tio Pepe*, Pedro Domecq, Sandeman and Williams and Humbert have free, comprehensive tours with English-speaking guides, and you will be able to taste the wines afterwards. In Puerto de Santa Maria, just a few kilometres away, there are tours at the *bodegas* of Fernando Terry and Osborne. Most tours take place in the morning between 10.00 and 01.30, and you do not need to make a prior booking for these. For other *bodegas* enquire at your hotel or at the tourist information in the centre of Jerez – at Alameda Cristina (tel: 956–34 20 37).

In the area which Marimar Torres classifies as the central zone, comprising Castile–La Mancha, there are some 2000 *bodegas* producing *vino de la mesa* (everyday table wine). Valdepeñas, which used to form part of La Mancha, is now a demarcated zone and is one of the most well-known names in table wine. Both red and white wines are produced and should be asked for as *tinto* or *blanco* respectively. In bars you are unlikely to be given any choice of *bodega* but on wine lists in restaurants you will find a variety on offer.

The central zone

Perhaps the most well-known quality wines of Spain are those from the Rioja area along part of the Ebro River, with the towns of Haro and Logroño, Cenicero and Fuenmayor being the important centres. There are some fifty-four *bodegas* in the region (many of which can be visited) producing both red and white wines. The bulk of the production is red wine which, aged in wooden casks, has a distinctively oaky 'nose' and flavour. The white wines are not aged in wooden casks and are light, fresh and fruity. Part of the Rioja area is in Navarre but it is only fair to mention that that region also produces its own wines, particularly the sturdy red table wines which are just becoming known outside of Spain, and is particularly famous for its *rosados* (rosés).

The northern zone

Rioja

There are so many *bodegas* you can visit in the Rioja region that it is impossible to list them here, so arrange your visits through the tourist information office at Miguel Villanueva 10, Logroño (tel: 941–21 54 97).

It is worth mentioning one very special wine which comes from the Upper Duero region near Valladolid,

The Upper Duero

and that is Vega Sicilia. There is a strictly limited production of this red wine and so it is difficult to find except in fine restaurants and hotels. The Vega Sicilia Valbuena is released after three or four years, but the *Unico* is kept on the estate for at least ten years. If you wish to visit the *bodegas* of Vega Sicilia either call directly (983–300393 or 220318) or ask at the tourist information office at Plaza de Zorilla 3, Valladolid (tel: 983–22 16 29), which will also be able to give you information about other *bodegas* in the Duero area.

Galicia   The famous demarcated area in Galicia is that of Ribeiro, where the best wines are white. Actually they are often referred to as 'green wines' and compared with the *vinhos verdes* of Portugal. They are highly distinctive because they have a slight, although noticeable, bubble to them. There is, however, a far greater production of reds, which have a very sharp and rough taste. In Galicia you are likely to be served them in miniature, shallow, white ceramic bowls; combined with the taste, this makes the drinking of red wine in this region an interesting experience. Because so much of Galician wine is consumed locally, what you drink in bars and restaurants will usually come in unmarked bottles and be from a small-scale producer.

Catalonia   Jan Read notes that the Catalans claim to make the greatest variety of wines of any region of Spain, ranging from the *rancios* (madeirized white wines which have a distinctive sherry-like bouquet, the best of which he compares with the matured Andalusian *olorosos*), fine table wines, sparkling wines, high quality brandy and other liqueurs. There is even a winery, that of De Muller, which is internationally famous for its altar wine. This range is highly appropriate for a region which is also renowned for the variety and quality of its cuisine.

The region of Penedes produces perhaps the highest quality red and white wines of the area, many of which have an international reputation. The red wines spend less time in the cask, so although full-bodied they are less oaky than the Riojas. An important centre of production is at Villafranca del Penedes (on the main road between Barcelona and Tarragona) where the most important *bodegas* are those of the Torres family, who make, among other wines, the notable Viña Sol and Esmeralda whites and the Sangre de Toro and Coronas reds. The Torres *bodega* can be contacted directly by calling 93–890 1000 or 890 2504, or by enquiring at the nearest major tourist office, at Gran Via de les Corts Catalanes 658, Barcelona (tel: 93–301 74 43).

Catalonia produces the majority and the best of the *cava* (sparkling wines) in Spain and of the hundred *bodegas* which produce this, eighty-three are in the Penedes area. Wine connoisseurs quite rightly insist that this should be regarded not as an inferior Spanish champagne but as a distinctive wine in its own right. The essential feature of its production, called *méthode champenoise*, is that the secondary fermentation in the bottle produces the sparkle. The *cavas* are classified as *bruto* (very dry), *seco* (dry), *semi-seco* (semi-dry), *semi dulce* (semi-sweet) and *dulce* (sweet). The two most important *bodegas*, both of which can be visited, are Codorníu (tel: 93–891 0125) and Freixenet (tel: 93–891 0125). Both are in San Sadurní de Noia, which is a few kilometres to the northeast of Villafranca.

Other drinks

Sangría

Unfortunately in many establishments *sangría* is little more than red wine and lemonade with some fruit thrown in, but if properly prepared it is a delicious summer punch of red wine, lemonade or soda, brandy, gin, fruit (particularly oranges and lemons), ice-cubes and perhaps cinnamon. A similarly refreshing, although simpler, warm-weather drink is *tinto de verano* (summer wine), which is red wine to which is added *casera* (lemonade).

Beer

Most Spanish *cerveza* (beer) is light and of the lager type, but it generally has more taste than many of the barrelled lagers found in British pubs. It is served either from the barrel or from the bottle and is usually cold, making it a very refreshing drink in the summer. Although different regions produce or stock different varieties, the most commonly available are Aguila, Cruz Campo, Estrella and San Miguel. There are a few dark beers produced, called *cerveza negra*.

Cider
The very best *sidra* is the sour cider produced in Asturias. Although this is now bottled and distributed all over Spain it is best drunk from the barrel in an Asturian bar, where you will be most likely to see the particular ritual involved with pouring and drinking it. The cider is usually decanted into bottles; the person serving will lift the bottle high and very slowly pour about a half glass per person – sticklers for tradition who want to show off will pour it over their shoulder into a glass held by their leg. The drinkers will then drink all but a small amount, the part which contains the sediment, which they throw on the floor.

Brandy
Although for legal reasons Spanish brandy cannot be labelled cognac it is called just that, *coñac*, in bars, and it is drunk by many people not only after lunch or dinner but also as part of a bar breakfast. Most Spanish *coñac* tends to be sweeter and heavier than the French varieties but there are exceptions. The biggest *coñac* production is in Jerez and there is a great variety to choose from. Soberano and Fundador are enormously popular and are less sweet than the caramelized Terry or Osborne *coñacs* produced in Puerto de Santa Maria. There are also more refined Jerez *coñacs* such as the Carlos range. Jan Read suggests that the *coñac* produced in Penedes by the *bodegas* Torres and Mascaró is the closest to French brandy in its lightness and dryness.

Anís *and* aguardiente
These are another couple of spirits with which many Spaniards shake their system into life at breakfast. *Aguardiente* is not less than 80 per cent proof and is usually made by distilling grape skins and pips. *Anís*, as the name suggests, is an aniseed-flavoured distillation based on the same grape leftovers. To order a glass, ask for *una copa de anís* or *una copa de aguardiente*. You will be asked if you would like it *seco* (dry) or *dulce* (sweet).

If you really wish to tell your system that it is somewhere different try *sol y sombra* (literally 'sun and shade' – the term is a bullfighting one), which is a mixture of *anís* and *coñac*. The most famous brand of *anís*, *Chinchon*, comes from the town of Chinchon near Madrid, and other popular varieties are those of the *Anís del Mono* brands. You will see that the labels of many *anís* bottles bear a picture of a bullfighter; this perhaps refers either to the courage necessary to drink it or to the courage which the drinking of it gives.

In Galicia there is a terrifyingly potent variety of *aguardiente* called *orujo* (the name refers to the grape mush from which it is distilled), which seems to be almost 100 per cent pure spirit, but it is a wonderfully satisfying and settling after-meal drink. In the same region there is a special way of drinking *aguardiente*, which consists of setting fire to a small bowl of it and drinking it when the flame has subsided; the resulting liquid is called *queimada*. Jan Read et al. in *The Wine and Food of Spain* report that one bodega describes its *aguardiente* as:

A drink which taken by itself requires three men to a glass: one to drink it and two friends to support him, since it is one of the strongest drinks in the world. If drunk in the form of *queimada*, it is transformed into a deceptively mild nectar, dangerous in the extreme by virtue of the spell it then casts. The *Cooperativistas* of Ribeiro recommend that before drinking it, you pin a card with your address on the lapel of your jacket.

Gin and rum are popular drinks in Spain, although gin more so than rum. The wonderful thing for drinkers of spirits is the measures which are served. You will not find bottles with the mechanism which liberates only enough drops to stain the bottom of a glass; the barman actually tips the bottle up and *pours a quantity* into the glass.

Gordon's Gin is available but the most popular are three Spanish brands, Larios, Rives and MG. They are usually drunk as *un gin tonic* or *una ginebra*

Ginebra *and* ron

con tónica (a gin and tonic). It is interesting that in the Basque region, where MG is more frequently asked for, Larios is regarded as an Andalusian gin. The result is that many Basques regard with concern a Spaniard in a Basque bar asking for a Larios, because many Andalusians serve in the paramilitary *guardia civil* and are posted to the Basque area, where the force is in the main unpopular and for many a threat to Basque nationalism. A person asking for a Larios is likely to be southern and thus, potentially, a police officer.

Rum is usually drunk with Coca Cola and is known as a *cuba libre* or a *cubata*. A *cubata* can also be a gin and tonic or gin and lemon, but you will usually have to ask for *una cubata de ginebra* to avoid a rum and coke.

Whisky Whisky drinkers are probably best advised to drink the well-known imported Scottish whiskies; the two most popular brands seem to be J & B and Ballantynes, which can be asked for by name. The Spanish produced DYC has little to recommend it, and it is certainly not very popular with the Spaniards. Once again the great thing about drinking whisky in Spain is the measures which are poured. It is usually served in a tall glass with ice, so while '*un whisky*' will suffice when you ask for the drink, if you want it without ice ask for *un whisky sin hielo*.

A word of warning: although it was mentioned earlier that wayside bars, restaurants and inns cater for the hungry and thirsty traveller it should not be assumed that the *wiskeries* on the outskirts of many towns are a haven for connoisseurs of Scotch, for these are in fact very down market semi-brothels.

Liqueurs Apart from the internationally known liqueurs such as Cointreau, Chartreuse and Benedictine, Spain produces several of its own such as Cuarenta y Tres, which Jan Read neatly describes as being similar to Southern Comfort, Ponche (usually coming in a distinctive metallic-looking bottle, and made of brandy and herbs), and Pacharan, made from bilberries. Bailey's, the Irish cream whisky liqueur, is also becoming popular – it is drunk long with ice.

Shopping

One of the great delights of shopping for food in Spain is that you are able to buy kilos of cheap fresh vegetables or fruit which, because of their cost, you would probably buy as individual items at home. Even if you are staying in a hotel on full board it is worth going to the local market or fruit and vegetable shop for extra fruit. Of course if you are having to feed yourself then this will be necessary, but it should not be regarded as an unpleasant chore on the margins of your holiday. It is much more fun and interesting if it is treated, as many Spaniards treat it (especially in small towns and villages), as a facet of social life.

Markets are generally open from 08.00 until about 12.00 and, apart from fruit and vegetables, will usually sell fresh meat and poultry, cured meats and fish. The range of products on sale will naturally depend on where you are in Spain and will reflect regional specialities (see the 'Food' chapter). The easiest way to make your purchases is to point to the item and ask for so many kilos, but you can also say *'Déme un kilo [dos kilos] por favor'* ('Give me a kilo [two kilos], please') or, for smaller amounts, *'cuarto kilo'* ('quarter kilo') or *'medio kilo'* ('half kilo'). If you want to know how much something costs you should ask *'¿Cuanto es?'*

Some of the more common vegetables and fruits are: *patatas* (potatoes), *tomates* (tomatoes), *lechuga* (lettuce), *pimientos* (peppers), *pepinos* (cucumbers), *apio* (celery), *cebollas* (onions), *zanahorias* (carrots), *ajo* (garlic), *berenjenas* (aubergines), *aceitunas* (olives), *naranjas* (oranges), *limones* (lemons), *manzanas* (apples), *plátanos* (bananas), *uvas* (grapes), *melocontones* (peaches), *albaricoques* (apricots), *melones* (melons) and *sandias* (watermelons). If you cannot find the local market then the place to look for is a *frutería*, which will sell both fruit and vegetables.

You should not be reticent in making your requests to the stallholder for if you wait to be served, as in a bar, you could wait for a long time. Patient queuing is not a highly developed art in Spain and you will find in most food shops that several customers will ask for things at the same time, and that the shopkeeper or stallholder will serve several people simultaneously. The advantage for the shopkeeper is that he or she can, as it were, hold onto customers in this way, for they cannot just leave for another establishment. Customers are generally, though, in no hurry to make their purchases quickly and leave. They ask for one or two things, chat, look around and then ask for the next couple of things on their list. The advantage for the visitor is that you will not be hurried by an impatient shopkeeper and you will have time to look about and decide what you need. The valuable contribution that you will make is that of providing for the locals an added detail in the minor social drama of shopping, and if you care to join in by asking about the products on sale you will soon be given plenty of advice about what to buy.

Other shops are generally open between 08.30 and 14.00 and then from about 17.00 until 19.00 or 20.30 in the summer. In many smaller towns and villages some of the shops are not immediately obvious, being in fact part of ordinary houses with the room giving onto the street being used as a shop. Of the shops selling foodstuffs, the main classifications are given below.

Panadería *or* despacho de pan	This is the baker's or breadshop. The generic name for bread is *pan* and most Spaniards buy it in the form of large individual rolls. The most common types are *viernas*, which are the long, wide and almost oval-shsaped rolls which are normally used for making the hefty *bocadillos* (sandwiches) served in bars, or *bollos*, which are smaller and round. Both of these bread rolls have a well-baked crust and are soft inside. A *barra* is like a short, french-style loaf.

In different parts of Spain you will come across different regional styles of loaves, usually large and round, and these are generally referred to simply as *pan*. The great advantage of these loaves is that the bread tends to be heavy and dense and so does not dry out very quickly. Wholemeal bread can be found in many parts of Spain and is known as *pan integral*. If you are looking for sliced processed bread, *pan de molde*, don't expect to find it here; go to a grocer's.

Pastelería *or* confitería

These pastry or cake shops are usually easily identified, for they will have a range of gateaux, fruit tarts, biscuits and various cream-filled monstrosities in the window. The generic name for a large cake is usually *pastel* or *tarta* (a birthday cake for example is a *tarta de cumpleaños*, a sponge is a *bizcocho*, biscuits are *galletas* and a tart or flan is a *torta*.

Many of the larger pastry shops have a bar within them or, more elegantly, a *salón de té* (a tea room) where you can consume the various products on sale.

Ultramarinos

These grocer's shops are usually the equivalent to a local, corner grocer's shop in Britain and carry the same range of products. The service is likely to be personal and the same rules for the market and vegetable shops apply here: don't expect to work quickly down your shopping list; start asking and look around at the same time.

Apart from canned and dried goods you will also find cheeses, hams and other cured meats in a grocer's. The best ham is mountain cured, *jamón serrano*. You will see legs of this hanging in the shops. The very best of this comes from the longest cured hams from wild pigs, which are known as *pata negra* (literally 'black foot' – see the 'Food' chapter). This ham will be cut wafer thin, and although expensive it is one of the great tastes of Spain. Industrially produced processed ham is *jamón de york*.

Different regions of Spain produce their individual styles of spiced sausages and cured meats. The most common is *chorizo*, somewhat like a coarse salami; others are *morcilla* (blood pudding); *morcon*, which is like *chorizo* but has an irregular shape; *caña de lomo*, (cured loin of pork prepared in a thick sausage shape) and *salchicha* (the generic name for sausage), the varieties of which often resemble breakfast sausages.

Some *ultramarinos* have moved away from counter service and have become small *supermercados*, where you serve yourself.

Carnicería
This is the butcher's shop. The range of meats on sale will very much depend on the region, and the best meats are probably to be found in the northern parts of the country. Although the generic name for meat is *carne*, this tends to mean beef. Other meats are pork (*cerdo*), chicken (*pollo*), turkey (*pavo*), duck (*pato*), lamb (*cordero*), veal (*ternera*), rabbit (*conejo*), suckling pig (*lechon*) and kid (*chivito*). Of the various cuts of meat the most common name for a steak is a *filete*, but a tenderloin is a *solomillo*, chops are *chuletas*, loin is *lomo*, a joint of roasting beef is usually a *redondo*, a shoulder is a *paleta* and a leg of lamb *una pata de cordero*. Kidneys are *riñones*, liver *higado* and sausages *salchichas* or *salchichones*. Hams and cured meats can also be bought in many butchers'.

Pescadería
These are fishmongers' shops. Once again, the variety and quantity of fish will vary from region to region, and although the Mediterranean coast is rich in fish (*pescado*) and shellfish (*mariscos*), the coastal regions of Galicia and the Basque country are justly renowned for the quantity and quality of their selection. Spaniards eat a great variety of fish and shellfish and it is difficult to list the creatures which are available, but the most common are hake (*merluza*), cod (*bacalao*), sole (*lenguado*), sea bass (*mero*), trout (*trucha*), swordfish (*pez espada*) which is bought in thick steaks, sardines (*sardinas*), young fresh anchovies (*boquerones*), red mullet (*salmonetes*), squid (*calamares*), octopus (*pulpo*), prawns (*gambas*) and oysters (*ostras*). With the fish which are sold whole

you might be asked whether you would like them
cleaned (*limpio*) or gutted (*destripado*).

These are supermarkets and hypermarkets. Shopping
in a supermarket has the advantage that you do not
have any language difficulties and you can shop at
your leisure. In recent years huge supermarkets
(*hipermercados*) have been established on the outskirts
of many large towns and cities, and they offer an
enormous range of food and domestic products.
Many of these *hipermercados* have a wonderful range
of fish, cheeses and meat products and usually a
wide variety of wines and spirits. If you have a car
and need to do a lot of food shopping it is well
worth considering doing it under one roof, but what
you lose, of course, is the atmosphere of the bustle
of the local markets and going from specialist shop
to specialist shop in the town centre.

Supermercado
and
hipermercado

Finally, you can find self-service food departments
in the famous department stores of *El Corte Ingles*
and *Galerias Preciados*, which are to be found in the
centre of major cities. Although the range of
foodstuffs does not have anything to recommend it
particularly as special, the advantage is that these
stores do not close for the afternoon *siesta*.

If you enjoy cooking then there are certain Spanish
products which are well worth taking home. Olive
oil (*aciete de oliva*) can be found cheap and of
excellent quality. The finest quality oil is known as
virgen and is made by a single cold pressing of the
olives. There are two grades of this oil, *extra* and
fino, both of which are green in colour. The grading
refers to the level of the acidity of the oil; *extra*, the
best, having the least acidity at less than 1 per cent,
and *fino* having less than 2 per cent. For some tastes
virgen oil is too pungent and many use it only for
salad dressings, but for those who like the flavour
this oil is wonderful to fry with. The other major
classification of olive oil is *refinado*; as the name
suggests this has been further refined and is then
blended with about 5–10 per cent of *virgen*. This
light yellow oil has a much lighter taste.

**Foodstuffs to
take home**

Olive oil is usually sold in plastic or glass bottles or in cans; beware of the slightly brittle plastic containers, because if you are not careful these can break in your luggage, and although olive oil does possess a wonderful aroma, having it in your clothes is probably not the best way to appreciate it. Olive oil can be bought directly from the mill (*la molina de aciete*), where it is usually sold by the kilo rather than the litre, but the mills are not easy to find, and you should head for a grocery shop or a supermarket where you will find a variety to choose from.

On the shelves close to the oils you will find olives (*aceitunas*). Once again there will be a variety to choose from. Not only do the olives vary in size but they also have differing flavours depending on the herbs and spices used in the liquid in which they are marinated. Markets and supermarkets (particularly in Andalusia where the greatest numbers of olives are grown, the finest of which are called *mazanilla* and *gorda*) are the places to look for local specialities in terms of their preparation; they are often sold from large tubs which allow you to taste the various kinds. *Ventas*, the roadside restaurants, often sell local produce, and large bottles of olives can be bought there.

The finest quality saffron (*azafrán*) in the world is harvested in Spain, and although expensive even there it is certainly cheaper than buying it in Britian. Saffron, the very best of which is called *La Mancha*, can be bought in most grocers in small plastic packets or perspex boxes. If you are lucky enough to find a herbalist's (*herbolario*) you can have these delicate threads weighed out for you, and this makes it somewhat cheaper. (If you buy it in threads you can be certain that it has not been cut with any other, similar-coloured powder.)

Spanish garlic (*ajo*) is usually of high quality with large, juicy and strongly flavoured cloves. An attractive and useful adornment for the kitchen at home is one of the plaited ropes of garlic (*una ristra de ajo*), which can be found on sale in markets, vegetable shops and supermarkets. Unfortunately it is obviously becoming less commercially viable to sell garlic in this way and it is more common to find it sold in plastic net bags; the quality is just as good but the presentation is not so attractive.

It is obviously worth while taking home your duty-free allowance of wines and spirits. Wines are often cheaper in supermarkets than in the duty-free shops of the airports and, except for the shop in Madrid airport, the range is probably greater in the larger supermarkets.

Other shopping

Tobacco

An *estanco* is a government licensed tobacconist's, easily recognized as such either by the yellow and dark red paintwork on the outside or by a similarly coloured sign. It is here that you will find the greatest range of cigarettes (*cigarillos*), cigars (*puros*) and pipe tobacco (*tabaco para pipas*). There are two basic classifications of cigarette tobacco, *tabaco rubio* (literally 'blond tobacco', which is Virginian) and *tabaco negro* ('black tobacco', which is a Turkish-style blend). International brands such as Benson and Hedges, Dunhill, Marlboro and Winston are readily available, but much more expensive than Spanish cigarettes. Probably the most popular Virginian tobacco cigarettes are Fortuna, and of the dark tobacco, Ducados or, more powerful still, Habanos. Cigars are good value, especially the Alvaro range, which are made in the Canaries, and the top-range Monte Cristo, which are Cuban. A good basic cigar, much favoured by truck drivers and available in most bars, is a Faria.

Cigarettes can also be bought in most bars and restaurants and these are easily visible on one of the shelves behind the bar, but many establishments now have automatic machines installed which carry a basic range of cigarettes. You will find kiosks (*kioscos*) in the street which sell most normal brands. Cigarettes bought in bars and *kioscos* tend to be slightly more expensive than those bought in *estancos*. If you do not wish to succumb to the temptation of having a whole packet, you can ask for one or two individual cigarettes at a kiosk or from the street vendors who circulate in the areas where there are many bars and restaurants.

Chemist's   See the chapter on 'Medical matters'.
(farmacia)

Bookshop and   Apart from books some *librerias* (bookshops) also
stationers   sell newspapers, but the usual place to look for these
is in the kiosks in the street. In the larger towns and
cities those near the centre will often carry a range
of foreign newspapers, and on the south coast, in
the main tourist resorts, you will also find Spanish-
produced English language newspapers which give
good local information. *Papelerías* (stationers) carry
the range of items that you would expect to find in
a British stationers – envelopes, writing paper, biros
etc – and many of them will have photocopying
facilities.

Department   The most famous chain of department stores is El
stores   Corte Ingles which has established itself in the major
cities. The incredible success of this chain has been
possible because of economic growth and the demand
of the middle classes for quality goods. So spectacular
has been the chain's expansion that, according to the
last available statistics, it ranked as the third most
important Spanish company in terms of sales. El
Corte Ingles has a very upmarket image and, apart
from internationally famous labels from the world
of fashion and design, you will also find many of
the best examples of Spanish products. The stores
are geared to the needs of foreign shoppers and
provide an interpreting service. As mentioned in the
chapter on 'Money matters', you can change money
and travellers' cheques out of banking hours at El
Corte Ingles.

Galerias Preciadas is another famous chain but it
does not have the image or the range of products of
El Corte Ingles.

Services   *Hairdressers* (peluquería *or* salón de belleza).   Given
the personal nature of the service it is very difficult
to give advice about coping in this situation. Words
such as *un recorte* (a trim), *un poquito* (a little), or

no mucho (not much) might be useful, though, when combined with the necessary gestures.

Laundry and dry cleaners (lavandería *and* tintoría). If you are staying in a hotel with these facilities you may want to ensure that something is *limpiado en seco* (dry cleaned) rather than *lavado* (washed). If you are looking for a launderette you should ask ('*¿Hay una lavadería automática por aqui?*') ('Is there a launderette nearby?'). Similarly, if you are looking for a dry cleaners you should ask for *una tintoría.* Useful phrases here might be ('*¿Cuándo estará lista?*' ('When will it be ready?') and '*La necesito. . .* ' ('I need it. . . ').

Spanish goods

Although lack of space does not allow the inclusion of all the Spanish goods and craft products which are worth looking out for, some do deserve special mention.

Spain has a large leather industry and many of the products are of the highest quality. Leather and suede coats, jackets and shoes are a particularly good buy, as are leather bags and wallets. The little village of Ubrique in the mountains east of Jerez is a very important leather centre and items can be bought cheaply there direct from the producers.

Mallorcan pearls are eagerly sought and are good value. The important centre of the industry is at Manacor. It would seem that the collectors of the internationally renowned pastel-shaded figurines of Lladró get particularly good bargains by buying them in Spain, even more so if they buy them direct from the factory exhibition shop near Valencia.

Inexpensive earthenware can be bought throughout Spain and each region produces its own distinctive pottery and ceramics. Talavera de la Reina in New Castile has a national reputation for its pottery and ceramics, and along the main road which passes through the town you will find dozens of shops with their wares displayed outside and advertising *exposition y venta* (exhibition and sale). Andalusian workshops too produce interesting ceramics, including particularly brightly coloured and ornate tiles.

Good examples of these can be found in Seville, a city which also produces finely embroidered shawls and *mantillas*.

Granada is famous for its ceramics and marquetry, Largatera (in New Castile) for its embroidery and Toledo for its damescene ware and other metalwork.

Sightseeing and entertainment

In recent years Spanish organizations have begun actively to recognize the importance of Spain's artistic heritage, and more money is being made available for restoration, conservation and presentation of its treasures. Generally, though, 'cultural tourism' is less developed than in other parts of Europe. Although you are likely to encounter crowds at key sites on the guided tour routes you are unlikely to come across the seething crowds to be found in the centre of Florence and in St Mark's Square in Venice, or the thousands which daily descend on Versailles in the summer. In many ways it is fortunate that the majority of the millions who visit Spain annually *do* only stay on the coasts and never venture into the Spain which is 'different' from the tourist board's publicity; it certainly makes it more pleasant for those who wish to explore churches, castles, galleries and museums.

Various guide books are recommended in the 'Preparations' chapter, these will obviously give you detailed information about the places you visit. There are some outstanding galleries ranging from the Prado in Madrid, which, apart from its international collection, has impressive collections of major Spanish artists such as Velásquez, Goya, El Greco, Zurbaran, Murillo and Ribera, to the specialist galleries such as the Museo-Teatro in Figueras dedicated to Dalí, the Picasso Museum in Barcelona and the Fundación Joan Miró, also in Barcelona. There are whole sections of towns such as Toledo and Cáceres which are conserved as national monuments, and there are truly special sights such as the Moorish palace of the Alhambra in Granada (one of the architectural wonders of Spain), the Roman remains in Merida, the fantastical architecture of Gaudi in Barcelona, El

Cultural visits

Escorial near Madrid, the Valley of the Fallen (the greatest monument to Fascism in Spain), the aqueduct at Segovia, the mosque and cathedral in Cordoba, and the central squares of Madrid, Salamanca and Aranjuez. Such a list, however, merely represents my prejudices.

Not only will you find a whole range of 'monumental' architecture – Roman, Visigothic, medieval Moorish, medieval Christian (and the mixture of Moorish and Christian), the major Europepan styles pre- and post-renaissance, neoclassical and on to the modern international styles in big cities – but you will also find an enormous range in 'popular' architecture. Regional identities are very strong in Spain and there are whole worlds of cultural difference between, for example, the *chozas* (straw-thatched huts) hidden away in the northern mountain areas, the sombre ochre villages with their burnt red-tiled roofs in central Spain, and the brilliant white villages of the south.

Sightseeing   The only real problem with visiting monuments, galleries and museums is the fact that, in most instances, they close in the afternoon, often between about 13.30 and 16.30, after which they open again for a couple of hours. This is often inconvenient for visitors who have not adjusted their systems to Spanish eating habits, but it does actually correspond to lunch time and the *siesta*. In the summer Spaniards do not like to be about in the often intense heat at this time of day, and if you have a hotel it is worth considering retiring for a *siesta* then. These opening times should not pose too much of a problem if you are actually staying in the town, but if you have made a special trip it can be frustrating and disappointing.

One problem which you might find if churches are your passion is that many, especially those which are not on the normal tourist circuit, are locked when services are not being conducted. If you are in a small town or village and really want to see the church ask for the *casa del cura* (the priest's house), which will be close by, and ask there. The best general advice for visiting major sights is that you

"Nowadays, every Tom, Dick and Harry seems to think they can stray off the tourist-route."

check in the latest edition of a guide book or ask at the local tourist office, but watch out for *their* eccentric opening times!

Charges

These vary enormously. In many of the major museums and galleries Spaniards enjoy free admission while foreigners pay, although the amount is usually modest. There are often reductions for students with international identification cards and for children. Cathedrals and monasteries also often charge a small admission fee.

Churches

It is important to emphasize here that you should dress appropriately. Many visitors are disappointed by being refused admission to cathedrals and churches because the ecclesiastical authorities disapprove of what they are wearing; the result of one group regarding the building as yet another 'sight' and the other regarding it as a place of worship. The rules are not strict and compliance is not onerous, but those in shorts or singlets will certainly be turned away, as will women whose tops are particularly scanty or whose skirts are very short. All the authorities ask is that you be decently covered, and if you are not in shorts or a short skirt it is easy to put on another layer over a top. Religious buildings which attract many visitors may well have rules which restrict visits when services are in progress, but in many others you will be able to enter at such times and it will be left to your own sense of appropriate behaviour to direct your visit.

Sightseeing tours
It is possible to book a variety of tours in major cities and from important tourist centres. City tours are certainly useful as a short orientation course to major sights in the city, which you can then come back to and explore at your leisure, but if you are going on a part- or whole-day tour to a particular location you really ought to ask how long you will actually spend seeing the things you want to see. Major tourist sights are also used as a chance to sell local handicrafts to visitors, and you may find that unscrupulous guides prefer to offer you the bargains of a local workshop, tourist shop or handicraft centre rather than explaining the castle, monastery or museum which is your main object of interest.

The paseo
The leisurely early evening or, at the weekend, midmorning stroll (the *paseo*) in the main streets and central squares is a delightful social occasion still much in evidence in smaller towns and villages, although somewhat obscured in the bustle of the larger cities. Here you will see Spaniards, dressed up to be seen to the best advantage in public, slowly walking in family groups, groups of friends or courting couples, with no particular aim other than that of being out in the street, of seeing and being seen, and of enjoying the company of their fellow human beings. They may stop to have a drink and a *tapa* or a coffee, but this is not to satisfy thirst or hunger; the custom is essentially an exercise in sociability.

For those visitors who are 'people watchers' this is a lovely time to sit at a pavement café or join the *paseo* and speculate on Spanish social life. Particularly fascinating is the show provided in villages and smaller towns by the single-sex groups of young friends, each of which watches the other and slowly makes contact.

In most towns and cities cinemas are open every day of the week and in the larger cities you will find that there are screenings from the early afternoon until about 22.30. Local newspapers will give details of the films (*peliculas*) which are showing and their times. The important national newspapers such as *El País, A.B.C,* and *La Vanguardia* have sections on the cinema in the capital, Barcelona and major Andalusian cities.

Going to the cinema is a cheap, popular form of entertainment, but you should expect to find that most cinemas will dub rather than subtitle foreign films. Although this can be annoying if all you want to do is escape into another world for a while, it is a wonderfully painless way of learning more Spanish, especially if it is a film you already know and you do not have to bother attempting to follow the storyline. Cinemas which are showing foreign films with subtitles will usually announce them with the letters *VO* (*voz original* – original soundtrack).

Information about theatres and concerts can also be found in the national neswspapers mentioned above, and you will find that the most important theatres are in Madrid and Barcelona. Once again, theatre tickets are inexpensive and for many productions you will find that there are performances in the early evening and again at about 22.00 or 22.30.

A ticket for the cinema or theatre is *una entrada* (literally 'an entrance').

Spanish television is controlled by the state and when it was first established during the Franco dictatorship it played a powerful role in propagating the views and image of the regime. Many Spaniards complain that it is still too tied to the government, and there are strong criticisms of the quality of its programming. Political issues aside, programmes do seem to be improving.

Of the channels, TVE1 has an emphasis on entertainment and music shows, with soap operas, children's shows, news/information and films fairly equally represented. TVE2 has more emphasis on sport and regional shows but with some series, films and documentaries. You will also find all-night TV on Saturday nights and it is possible that this will be extended to the rest of the week. Once again, because of the importance of regional identity there has been a strong development of regional programmes (in the regional language if it exists), and there are now special channels in the Basque country, Catalonia, Galicia and Andalusia, with more to come in Valencia and Madrid.

In many parts of Spain you will be able to tune in to satellite channels – Sky Channel, Super Channel, Children's Network and Lifestyle – which have English language programmes. Details of programmes can be found in newspapers, in more detail in the weekly supplements of major newspapers, and in specialist television magazines on sale at news-stands.

Apart from national radio stations, which offer a whole range of programmes including news, discussion and popular and classical music, there also hundreds of local stations. Programmes in English can be tuned in to if you are near American military bases such as those in Rota (Cadiz), Madrid and Zaragoza. In Mallora there is a station which broadcasts in English, except at midday and in the early evening, on 103.2 FM, and Radio 80 (89 FM) in Madrid has an English language programme between 06.00 and 08.00 every day except Sunday.

Discotecas   Even quite small villages seem to have their disco-theques these days, so it is very easy to find somewhere to dance the night away. Except for some of the more exclusive establishments in Barcelona and Madrid discotheques have very low entrance fees, and this fee usually allows you one free drink

of any kind. Some discotheques, especially in villages
and small towns, are really little more than large bars
with music and a dance floor; they do not charge
for admission but the drinks will probably be a little
more expensive than in other bars. They are certainly
one of the places to go if you want to meet Spanish
young people.

As Spaniards rarely dress in a scruffy manner when
they go out in public there are seldom monsters at
the door checking on what you are wearing before
allowing you in, and you should certainly have no
problems entering in even the most casual of clothes.
The exception to this is in some heavily touristed
areas where there have been problems with drunkenness and violence. Here the doormen may actually
be employees of local security firms and are often
armed with night sticks. They represent a sad
comment on the influence of some forms of tourism.

Discotheques in the south can be quite surprising
in that several times during the night the main lights
will come on and scores of couples will rush onto
the floor to dance *sevillanas* (a popular *flamenco*-
style dance); a peculiarly formal interlude in an
evening of free-form gyrations.

If you want to see a football match the season is a   *Football*
long one, from August to June. It is not usually
difficult to get tickets, except for important cup
matches, and the prices are not very different from
those in Britain.

Sport and leisure

Mass tourism is associated with the coastal regions of Spain, and the Spain of high mountains, barren plateaux, woodlands and national parks is generally little known. For those who are seeking neither a holiday exploring Spanish culture nor the relaxation of the beaches, Spanish topography offers a wide range of opportunities for hikers, climbers, horse-riders, naturalists, those who wish to hunt and fish, skiers, and golfers.

Hiking and climbing
One of the problems of preparing a hiking or climbing trip is that this sort of small-scale tourism has not really entered the purview of the national tourist board, so in order to obtain the necessary information you need to contact the appropriate local organizations and clubs, and this can be somewhat difficult. One way to avoid these problems is to arrange an all-inclusive outdoors holiday in the particular area you want to visit; the travel sections of newspapers now carry advertisements from many companies which specialize in these. If, however, you intend to make your own arrangements there is one handbook, *On Foot Through Europe: A Trail Guide to Spain and Portugal* by Craig Evans (Quill 1982), which is invaluable. Evans gives details of walking and climbing areas, lists of the various maps which are available and all the addresses of the specialist clubs which can give advice and information to you.

For those who wish to explore the highlands of Spain there are five main mountain chains on the Spanish peninsula, each of which is composed of individual mountain ranges or *sierras*. Along the French border is the largest single mountain range in Europe, the Pyrenees; across northern Spain is the Cantabrian Chain; the Central Mountain System contains the Sierra de Gredos and the Sierra de Guadarrama; running southeast from Burgos and Logroño is the Iberian System; and in the south is the Penibetic System, which includes the Sierra Nevada and, a little further to the northeast, the Sierra de Cazorla.

In order to explore these areas you will need to equip yourself with specialist maps, and for a detailed listing of these you are advised to refer to Evans. Basically, though, the Mapa Topográfico Nacional de España series covers all of Spain, with sheet maps on a scale of 1: 50,000 which are detailed enough to show most footpaths and tracks. There are also more detailed walking maps available for each of the mountain areas.   *Maps*

Further information can be obtained from the National Geographic Institute (Institute Geografico Nacional), the Spanish Mountaineering Federation, and the specialist bookshop Llibreria Quera in Barcelona, which operates a mail-order service for hiking and mountaineering guide books and maps. The addresses are given below.

Refugios (mountain huts or refuges) are to be found in many of the main mountain areas and are available for those who need overnight shelter when hiking. Although some are staffed in the spring and summer and can supply food, most are not and you will need to have sleeping bags, cooking equipment and food with you. Many of the huts are kept locked and to be able to obtain the keys you either need to be a member of a hiking association or to get information about access from the local controlling organization affiliated to the Spanish Mountaineering Federation. If you write to this organization they will send you a list of all the *refugios*. They are listed according to mountain areas and in each entry there is information (in Spanish) about the exact location, the number of spaces, the facilities offered and, if it is not staffed, where to obtain the key.   Refugios

Useful   Maps can be obtained through:
addresses

Instituto Geográfico Nacional
Calle General Ibañez de Ibero 3
Madrid 3
Spain
Tel: 91–233 38 00

but perhaps more easily through this bookshop:

Llibreria Quera
Petritoxl 2
Barcelona 2
Spain
Tel: 93–318 07 43

to whom letters may be written in English.

The Spanish Mountaineering Federation is:

Federación Español de Montañismo
Alberto Aguilera 3 4^{OiZ}
Madrid 28015
Spain
Tel: 91–445 13 82 or 445 14 38

Riding   Although there are many places which rent horses
for day trips, there is one organization which has
specialized in long-distance treks through Spain on
horseback. They offer trips which last anything from
a weekend to a month in various parts of the country.
The longer routes follow itineraries with particular
themes, such as the smugglers' trails in Cadiz,
the villages and towns of the conquistadores in
Extremadura or the transhumance (seasonal pastoral
migration) routes from Trujillo into the Sierra de
Gredos, as well as other mountain and coastal trails.
If you enjoy being on horseback then this sort of
travelling is ideal for getting into lesser-known parts
of Spain.

For information you can write (in English) to:

Caminos and Caballos
Duque de Liria 3

Madrid 28015
Tel: 91–242 31 25 or 242 45 57

For those interested in natural history there are nine
major national parks (and a further twelve natural
parks) in very different parts of Spain.

**National
parks**

The oldest, founded in 1918, is that of Covadonga
in the province of Asturias. The park occupies part
of a mountainous region and is home to chamois,
wild boar, wolf, wildcat and bear as well as the more
common squirrel, badger and smaller mammals. In
the Pyrenees, in the province of Huesca, is the
Ordesa National Park, whose interesting wildlife
includes chamois, boar, eagles, vultures and falcons.
Also in the Pyrenees, in Lerida, is the national park
of Aigües Torts and the Lake of San Mauricio.
Famed for its lake and waterfall scenery, it is
particularly important for its flora.

Near Ciudad Real in La Mancha, at the confluence
of the rivers Guadiana and Cigüela, is the wetlands
park of Tablas de Damiel, a sanctuary for many
species of migrating birds and a breeding area for
aquatic species. Finally, on the peninsula, is the
massive (some 750 square km) wildlife reserve of the
Coto Doñana in the far southwest, on the delta of
the Guadalquivir river. As well as marshy areas, this
park has stable dry land and sandy dunes, and
consequently has a range of wildlife. It too is an
important wintering ground for migrating birds, but
it also has resident populations of flamingo, vultures
and the rare imperial eagle. Among the mammals it
is home to wild boar, deer and the rare Pardel lynx.
Particularly good Landrover tours, lasting some four
hours and conducted by trained specialists, can be
booked at the park offices.

In the Canaries there are four national parks. On
La Palma, near Santa Cruz de la Palma, is La
Caldereta de Taburiente. Although it does not have
any particularly significant wildlife it does have
unique plantlife associated with the well-conserved
Canaries pine forests. On Tenerife is the park of
Tiede, situated in a highland volcanic area which has
not only spectacular volcanic rock formations but

also a very special range of flora. On Lanzarotte the Timanfaya National Park is famous for the spectacular volcanic scenery, which resulted from eruptions in the eighteenth and nineteenth centuries. From the village of Yaiza you can arrange camelback excursions to the Montaña de Fuego (Fire Mountain), and along the Route of the Volcanoes on the islet of Hilario. The last national park to be found in the Canaries is that of Garajonay on the island of Gomera. This is a heavily wooded park and the aim has been to conserve the unique flora which, millions of years ago, was extensive throughout the Mediterranean area.

In all of these national parks the controlling organization has established visitors' centres where you can see exhibitions, collect material and often arrange guided tours. Should you wish to obtain more detailed information about any of them you can write in English to the National Institute of Nature Conservation (ICONA):

ICONA
Sección de Parques Nacionales
Gran Vía de San Francisco 35
28071
Madrid
Spain

Hunting and Fishing
(*Caza y Pesca*)

Hunting, and here the reference is to shooting, is popular in many parts of Spain, particularly for big game in the mountain areas and for game birds in many others. The range of big game attracts many foreigners, for they are able to hunt the large Spanish mountain goat, the big horned mountain sheep, various species of deer, wild boar and chamoix or ibex. Birds include pheasant, partridge, quail, grouse (especially a large species called the capercaillie) and a variety of water fowl. For visitors who wish to practise this sport it is probably easiest to arrange through one of the specialist agencies, which organize visits to particular reserves and estates dedicated to it, but it is certainly possible to make the necessary arrangements yourself. Hunting is possible in the national parks controlled by ICONA, but this is highly supervised and you must apply for the necessary permits and visits through them (address below). Sporting guns may be brought into Spain, but you must declare them, show your firearms certificate (with a Spanish translation) and obtain a temporary licence from the police at the point where you enter Spain.

If you wish to fish (*pescar*) in rivers which are not privately owned you will also need a permit, which can be obtained through the national parks authority whose address is given below. If you write in English make sure that the words *permiso de caza* (hunting permission) or *permiso de pesca* (fishing permission) appear in your letter.

Jefatura Provincial del ICONA
Licencia Nacional de Caza y Pesca
Jorge Juan 39
Madrid 1
Spain
Tel: 91–225 59 85

Skiing

Spain is the second most mountainous country in Europe and consequently offers may opportunities for winter skiing holidays, and it is certainly worth considering these as an alternative to the traditional European centres. Given that many of these centres are close to important cities you can easily combine healthy and vigorous physical activity with more leisurely cultural excursions and, perhaps less healthy, investigations of local gastronomy.

There are six major zones of Spain where winter sports can be pursued. In the Catalonian Pyrenees there are twelve major centres, of which the most notable – Nuria, La Molina, Masella and Baqueria-Beret – are close to the cities of Barcelona, Lerida and Gerona. The Aragonese Pyrenees have five main centres, of which Formigal and Candanchú are near the major cities of Huesca and Jaca. In the Cantabrian range along the northern coast there are six main centres, which include the stunning Picos de Europa, within the Covadonga National Park. All of these centres are easily reached from the coastal cities of Santander, Gijón, La Coruña and Vigo, as well as from Santiago and Bilbao, which have international airports.

The Iberian System runs in a north–south direction from the Cantabrians and has three centres near Logroño, Burgos and Teruel. The advantage of these centres is that, although they offer up-to-date facilities, they are in little known areas. The Central System has four centres close to the cities of Madrid, Segovia and Avila; the centre of Navacerrada is only 62 km from the capital – an hour's drive. The Penebetic System in the south has the winter sports centre of the Sierra Nevada, Europe's most southerly ski resort, where you can ski from December to May. It is only 32 km from Granada and about 103 km from the Mediterranean coast. This is an important resort and the Spanish Federation of Winter Sports certainly regard it as such, for they are making an application for its candidacy for hosting world skiing championships for 1992/3.

A general outline of skiing in Spain can be found in the brochure *Winter Sports in Spain*, which can be obained from the Spanish National Tourist Board. The Spanish Ministry of Tourism produces a more detailed booklet entitled *El Turismo de Nieve en España*, and although this is in Spanish the tables and information are readily understandable. It gives maps of access to the resorts, details of the types of run, prices for the use of ski lifts, prices for courses (as agreed by the General Assembly of the Ski School of Spain) and a list of hotels and their prices in the area.

Useful addresses
Spanish Winter Sports Federation
Federación Española Deportes de Invierno
Modesto Lafuente 4
Madrid
Spain
Tel: 1–446 91 18 or 446 99 68

The following organizations will also send booklets about different skiing areas:

Asociación Turística de Estaciones de Esqui y
Montaña
Juan Ramón Jiménez, 8
(Edificio Eurobuilding)
Madrid 28035
Spain
Tel: 91–458 15 57 or 458 75 26

British Ski Association
118 Eaton Square
London SW1W 9AF
UK
Tel: 01–245 1033

Golf

Golf is becoming ever more popular and every year
scores of new courses are being added, some of
which are of a high enough standard for international
tournaments. One of the great advantages of the
majority of Spanish courses is that they are in fine
condition when other northern European courses are
not, particularly in the early spring, autumn and
winter. It is significant in terms of the importance
of golf tourism that the vast majority of courses are
along the Mediterranean coast, so that golfing can
be combined with warm weather and relaxing. The
two other major centres are in the Madrid area and
on the Basque part of the northern coast.

As with other sports mentioned in this section
travel agents are able to offer special holidays for
golf, but if you wish to arrange them yourself the
Spanish National Tourist Board will send you a map
of all the golf courses with a list of various clubs.
The Royal Spanish Golf Federation (address below)
produces a booklet which not only gives information
about the courses and clubs but also lists all the
competitions for that year.

Real Federación Española de Golf
Capitan Haya, 9–5°. Sur
Madrid 28020
Spain
Tel: 91–455 27 57 or 455 26 82

Beaches and water sports

With some 8000 km of coastline, ranging from rocky shorelines with small sandy bays through river estuaries to long fine sandy beaches, Spain has plenty to choose from, and you certainly do not have to put up with the sort of monstrous coastline development found along parts of the Costa del Sol. It is true, however, that the majority of facilities for sports such as waterskiing, paraskiing and windsurfing are to be found in the larger tourist centres. Many people of course take the necessary equipment with them, and they are less dependent on such centres.

Windsurfing is particularly popular in the southwest corner of Andalusia, and the little town of Tarifa and its surrounding area seem to have become an important European centre. Further around the coast, on the Atlantic side, the larger waves and the bays make a good surfing area.

Details of watersports centres can be obtained from:

Federación Española de Esqui Nautico
Saino de Arana 30 1º 1ª
08028 Barcelona
Spain
Tel: 93–330 89 03

Sunbathing

Topless sunbathing is now a regular and accepted feature on most Spanish beaches and is unlikely to lead to any brushes with the law or with offended locals. It should certainly not be imagined that Spanish women are still a product of their conservative past, and there are plenty of them who are desirous of an all-over tan. Total nudity is less common, although not rare, but you might run the risk of causing what is known as *un escándolo público* (literally a public outrage or scandal), but this is more likely to be a complaint against those who are behaving in a sexually suggestive manner.

Swimming pools

If you are away from the coast and want to swim and cool off then look for the open-air *piscina* (swimming pool). Many towns and even small villages have them. Here it is unlikely that topless sunbathing would be acceptable.

Festivals

Whether at a national or a local level festivals are of enormous importance in the cultural and social life of Spain. There are well over 3000 such celebratory occasions, ranging from the internationally known San Fermines with the bullrunning in Pamplona, the Holy Week parades and the April Fair in Seville, the night-time madness of fireworks and burning parade floats in Las Fallas in Valencia, to the modest and intimate one-day patron saint celebrations of the smallest villages.

Such days are of fundamental importance to the communities which hold them – they are eagerly looked forward to and, when they arrive, eagerly and fully lived. Whether they have as their focus a religious procession, traditional competitions, a parade, a bullfight, bonfires and fireworks or singing and dancing, what they all share is a special intensification of social life, with people in the streets day and night. Such festivals depend on people 'living' them, generating the necessary spirit of *feria* or *fiesta*, so that an atmosphere of celebration pervades the community.

Some festivals are solemn and involve people coming together on the street to witness a spectacle such as the Holy Week processions, when enormous candle-lit floats with statues of the Virgin or Christ are carried or pulled through the crowded streets, accompanied by the somewhat sinister shrouded penitents (in what look like Ku Klux Klan costumes) and mournful bands. Others need there to be more active participants – when the bulls are run through the streets in Pamplona or young bulls are turned loose in the central square of a village. All but the most religious festivals involve convivial drinking and eating, singing and dancing, and the sheer enjoyment of being together in a noisy crowd.

Festival atmosphere

Festival is an atmosphere which visitors are easily able to tap into. Of course in the larger celebrations you are likely to remain a spectator, as are many of the visiting Spaniards. For example, on the last night of the April Fair in Seville there are easily a million people in and around the fairground, and San Fermin in Pamplona attracts enormous numbers of foreigners. In smaller celebrations, however, where you are more 'visible', you can become more intensely involved. In smaller towns and villages you are unlikely to be reacted to as intrusive – the local people are usually welcoming because they want people to think well of their locality. If you arrive at such a time, show yourself willing to take part, ask about it and are obviously enjoying yourself, you will certainly be drawn into it, and the locals will delight in making you feel part of it.

Don't, however, expect to feel rested if you want truly to live a *feria* or *fiesta* – most require an enormous expenditure of energy to cope with the crowds, noise, talk, dancing and, above all, the long hours of drinking (although it must also be said that there is rarely unpleasant drunkenness) and the very late nights. All of this requires a very special 'coping with Spain', but if you have a chance to join in a festival you will meet Spaniards at their most hospitable and exuberant.

Local and national festivals

With over 3000 to choose between it would be unfair to select only a few festivals for special mention. When in Spain ask at the local tourist offices to see if there is anything going on in the area or, if you wish to plan ahead, write to the Spanish National Tourist Office and ask for their booklets *Celebrating in Spain* and *Festivals of Special Interest to Tourists*.

Public holidays

As well as these local celebrations there are also the national public holidays listed below (when banks are closed), many of which are marked by special events.

January 1	New Year's Day
January 6	Epiphany – Day of the Kings

March 19	St Joseph's Day
April (variable date)	Maundy Thursday (except Barcelona)
April (variable date)	Good Friday
April (variable date)	Easter Monday (Barcelona and Palma de Mallorca only)
May 1	Labour Day
May/June	Corpus Christi (always a Thursday about six weeks after Easter Sunday)
June 24	King Juan Carlos's saint's day
July 25	St James's Day (patron saint of Spain)
August 15	Assumption Day
October 12	Day of Hispanidad/ Columbus Day (except Barcelona)
November 1	All Saints' Day
December 6	Constitution Day
December 8	Day of the Immaculate Conception
December 24	Christmas Eve (half day)
December 25	Christmas Day

The romantic image: flamenco and the bullfight

Flamenco The popular, romantic image of Spain being peopled by flamenco-singing and -dancing gypsies and swaggering bullfighters is unrealistic, but flamenco does occupy an important place in Spanish culture, although more particularly in Andalusian culture. It is not simply a preserved folkloric element, but rather a vibrant and important art of song and dance. It is certainly true that a version of flamenco has been commercialized and turned into a sanitized spectacle, but this bears little relation to the raw vigour of the true thing.

The problem for the visitor is where to see and hear the real thing. To find *cante jondo* (literally 'deep song'), which is the authentic, heart-rending sound of flamenco, or its other 'pure' forms you will need to enquire as to whether there is a *peña flamenca* (a flamenco club) or *un bar donde se canta flamenco* (a bar where flamenco is sung) nearby, but you are only likely to find these in Andalusian towns. Alternatively you can look for a more commercial *tablao flamenco* (flamenco show). Again, many of the larger Andalusian cities such as Seville, Cordoba and Granada have such establishments, and in Sacramonte, the gypsy area of Granada, you will find many. *Flamenco* shows are also staged in large cities such as Madrid and Barcelona. The problem with the commercial establishments is that you might be given a bland rendition of the various elements of the art, but many, it must be said, do give good value.

If you are in the south during the late spring and summer try to discover where the local *ferias* (festivals) are, for there you will be able to experience a version of flamenco song and dance, the *sevillana*. Even in the smallest villages you will find dozens of

"Right, the scene is set... release the mosquetos, Bernard."

groups of people, many in costume, singing and
clapping out the rhythm while the dancers wind
themselves around each other in what can only be
described as a controlled and highly stylized erotic
dance.

Although this is not the place to discuss fully the
morality of the bullfight, it is worth making a couple
of points. Most foreigners are aware that in the
bullfight several bulls are going to be injured in
various ways; they will be lanced, they will have
sharp barbs stuck in them and they will be killed
more or less efficiently with a sword; there will be
blood and there will be death. If you do not want
to see this, if you think you will be upset by it and
if you think it is barbaric and cruel, then it is really
not worth going because you will certainly not enjoy
it. You do not *need* to see a bullfight to know that
you are not going to like it or to have your opinions
confirmed about it and those who go to see it; there
are plenty of other ways to spend a pleasant spring
or summer afternoon in a Spanish town.

That said, the bullfight is a fascinating dramatic
event which can be both enormously exciting and
moving, and the elements of blood, suffering and

The bullfight

*To go or not
to go?*

death are less noticeable than might be imagined; they are certainly not central features in the event for Spaniards. If you approach it in a spirit of interested curiosity you will probably be engrossed by the complexities of a great Spanish drama.

Finding a Bullfights take place from early spring to autumn.
bullfight They are often held as part of the celebrations of major town fairs, such as Las Fallas in Valencia (at the beginning of spring, before Easter), La Feria de Abril (April Fair) in Seville, San Isidro in Madrid (after 15 May), San Fermin in Pamplona (starting 7 July) and the Feria de Pilar in Zaragoza (after 12 October), and in these major fairs as well as many others bullfights will be held on several afternoons. On these occasions you can see the greatest Spanish *matadores* (bullfighters) perform.

Bullfights are also often held as part of the annual celebrations of smaller towns and villages, and if you are visiting a town when its *feria* is taking place it is worth asking '*¿Hay toros?*' (literally 'Are there bulls?' but meaning 'Is there a bullfight?') or being on the lookout for posters advertising the event.

In larger cities such as Seville, Madrid and Barcelona bullfights are also held on a weekly basis. Once again, be on the lookout for posters in bars or on the street, or ask at your hotel or the tourist office.

The posters will announce whether it is to be a *corrida de toros* (a bullfight with four–six-year-old bulls and with senior *matadores*) or a *novillada* or *corrida de novillos* (with younger bulls and junior *matadores*). Do not be put off by this technical distinction, because only those who know the event really well can tell the difference and both events have exactly the same elements.

The posters will also give the place, date and time of the bullfight. The bullring is *la plaza de toros*; do look at the place-name because posters will announce bullfights in nearby towns and villages. They usually take place on a Sunday and always in the late afternoon or early evening. It is often said that bullfights begin at five o'clock in the afternoon (a popular poem by García Lorca seems to have given rise to this piece of information) but this is not always so – it depends on the heat at that time of year and the time of the setting sun. Bullfights are held in the coolest part of the day and at a time when there is still sufficient light; so, for example, in the south in midsummer they are often held at 7 p.m.

The other information given on the poster is the name of the ranch supplying the bulls and the names of the *matadores*. The *matadores* will be listed in their order of seniority and they will perform in that order.

Getting tickets

If you are staying at a hotel which acts as an agent for bullfight tickets then probably the easiest way of buying them is through the reception desk, but you will certainly pay a commission for this service. Tickets can also be bought at some bars and kiosks. They will announce the fact with a small banner, flag or poster with a bullfight scene and the words *billetes* (tickets) and *los toros* (the bullfight) displayed. Once again, though, if you buy tickets in this way you will pay a commission.

If you are planning to see a bullfight during one of the major fairs when there are several afternoons of fights, then try to buy your tickets from the *taquilla* (ticket office) at the bullring a day or so in advance. If you are buying a ticket (*una entrada*) on the day of the fight, get to the ticket office as early as possible during the day, to avoid the inevitable last-minute rush in the afternoon.

Ticket touts In towns where there are large numbers of tourists who are likely to attend bullfights there will be ticket touts outside the bullring or along the main approach roads to it. Ignore them (difficult, because they are persistent) and go to the ticket office. Often the touts will say that there are no tickets left, but do not take their word for it. If there are none, there will be a sign at the office saying *No hay billetes* (No tickets).

Should you decide to buy from the touts, it is up to you to negotiate a favourable deal. If there are

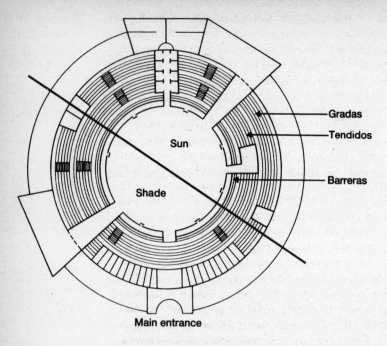

Schematic outline of building

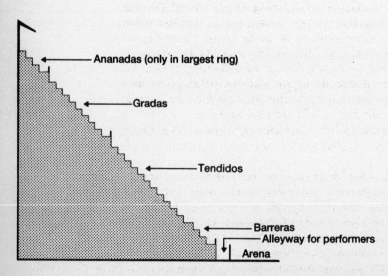

Schematic outline of seating in a bull ring.

still touts selling at the last moment then you might well be able to pick up a cheap ticket from them. If it is a sell-out fight at a major *feria* and there are exceptional bullfighters then the black-market tickets can fetch exceptional prices.

The major distinction between the seats in a bullfight is that between those in the *sol* (sun) and those in the *sombra* (shade). There are also tickets called *sol y sombra* (sun and shade), which are for seats that start in the sun but are in the shade by the middle of the event. *Sol* tickets are much cheaper than *sombra*, but you will be both squashed and hot, and most of the activity takes place on the *sombra* side of the arena. If you want to be comfortable, watch the preparations of the *matadores* and their teams and see the performance at closer range, it is worth buying one of the *sombra* seats.

Where to sit

You will also have to decide in which section to sit; this is a little more difficult to explain because different bullrings give different names to the seating areas. The illustration shows the most common names, but it must only be treated as a general guide to the major divisions.

My advice is, if you are going to attend just one bullfight, that it is worth paying for one of the higher seats in the shade – in the first row of *grada*, say (you would ask for '*la primera fila en grada de sombra*') – rather than a *tendido* in the sun. Of course if you are happy with the ticket prices then go for *barreras* in *sombra*, and ask for '*una entrada cerca de donde las cuadrillas ponen sus capotes*' ('a ticket near where the teams put their capes'); this is the central point of the action.

If you have left yourself enough time before the fight (allow yourself about fifteen or twenty minutes to get into the bullring and get yourself seated) you will be able to enjoy the atmosphere which begins to build up outside the bullring. If you wish to respect Spanish tradition and etiquette then shorts, singlets or beach wear are not appropriate. The bullfight is a fairly formal occasion, although you

Before the bullfight

will not be refused admittance if you are dressed like this. To be fully prepared for participation you ought to take a handkerchief with you; these are waved by the public to ask the president to award the bull's ears to a *matador* who has performed particularly well. Handkerchiefs should be white (and preferably clean); the colour because it is traditional, the cleanliness because you will be waving it under your neighbour's nose.

There are several other things which can be bought outside the bullring to equip you for a total bullfight experience. Cigars are an important part of the tradition (and add to the general discomfort in a packed bullring), and these can be bought at small stalls which sell cigarettes, cigars and sweets. Alvaro Brevas (cigars made in the Canaries) are particularly good and inexpensive; they are smooth, with plenty of taste but not too strong. An Alvaro is a 'three-bull cigar' – it is difficult to keep one going longer than that. For a cigar to take you through all six bulls you really need to go up market and buy a large Cuban cigar, an Habana; Monte Cristos are good but quite expensive.

Red carnations for the buttonhole, blouse or hair also indicate that you regard this as a special occasion. Other stalls will offer you cardboard sunshades (not necessary if you are in *sombra*), fans, sunflower seeds (these are useful because if you cannot bear some part of the action then you can always look down and shell the seeds), sweets and drinks.

Apart from the ticket touts, the most persistent people outside major bullrings are the poster sellers. The bullfight posters they have to offer are not official posters; they are printed simply for the tourist market. If you do decide to buy one as a souvenir of the bullfight then make sure that the names on the poster correspond to those on the official posters. It is worth remembering that El Cordobes has not been active as a bullfighter for well over ten years, so avoid those with his name, and if you are offered one with Manolete and El Cordobes featured together, look elsewhere – Manolete died while El Cordobes was still only a young boy. A final point:

it is worth buying your poster after the event. You might even get a reduction on the price because it is now out of date, and it does avoid getting it crushed in the crowd in the arena.

Allow yourself plenty of time to find your way to your seat in the larger bullrings, because you have to work out which gate to go in by, and then the section of the arena and the row of your seat. The ticket may tell you which *puerta* (gate) you should enter by, but if it does not then look at your section name and number – *tendido 11* or *grada 5* for example – for these should be indicated over one of the outside gates.

Finding your seat

As you go in you will probably find people renting cushions. It is worth paying to have one because your seat will be unpadded stone, brick or concrete and anyway the small amount you pay will go to the Red Cross. Once you have passed the barriers which allow you into the seating areas you must find your section, *fila* (row) and *asiento* (seat). It is certainly worth tipping (a tip of 25 pesetas should be enough) one of the porters or ushers to take you there. In that way you will actually get to the place allocated to you and he will remove anyone who has moved into your spot, something which is a common occurrence. If you do not have an usher with you and there is someone in what you think is your seat then it is best to show your ticket to them, and if they still do not move show it to someone nearby, plead *'¡Por favor!'* ('Please!') and attempt to enlist their support.

One of the advantages of arriving early is that you will not have to fight your way across and along rows and, once seated yourself, an amusing way to spend the time before the start is to watch how latecomers attempt to get to their seats (or what they think are their seats) and what they do when they find them occupied. Your space on the row will be about 45 cm wide and there is not much leg room, so expect to be a bit squeezed in and to have knees in your back and a back wedged between your knees. Judicious wriggling should sort out a reasonable relationship between you, the person in front and the one behind.

After the death of each bull it is a good idea to stand up and stretch a little, but try to sit down again before your neighbours; it helps put you in a commanding position.

There are no programmes for the bullfight so a few pointers as to how the event will progress are useful.

The main characters

The bulls Six bulls are fought in a normal bullfight. These are not domestic animals which have been maltreated to make them aggressive; they are a breed of wild bulls which are raised on specialist ranches. In a herd in the fields they are tranquil but once isolated and in a closed space they are fearsome. They are fast, deadly accurate with their horns and have so much strength that they can lift a man as though he were a rag doll.

The humans Three teams perform during the afternoon. Each of them consists of: a *matador*, who is the main performer and will kill two of the bulls; three *banderilleros*, his foot assistants who help him with their capework and who also stick the *banderillas* (coloured sticks) into the bulls; and the two *picadores*, who are mounted on heavily padded horses and armed with a metal-tipped lance which they use to stab the bull.

The *matadores* perform in order of seniority (determined by the date on which they were registered as full *matadores* with their union), not in order of fame or popularity. Each *matador* will fight two bulls. The senior man will take the first and fourth, the next most senior the second and fifth, and the last the third and sixth. It is often difficult to tell which are the *matadores* and which are the assistants, but the general rule is that the *matadores* have gold embroidery on their costumes whereas the assistants have silver.

The performance

At the appointed hour the president (the man who controls the bullfight) will take his seat in the presidential box and signal for the event to start. The band strikes up a *pasodoble* (a two-step dance/march) and the procession begins to form up in the arena. Two mounted constables in ceremonial dress cross the arena to a point below the presidential box and formally ask for permission to lead out the procession. These constables are responsible for checking that the rules are adhered to during the afternoon and they ensure that the president's decisions are carried out. They return to where the bullfighters are lining up and they lead out the procession.

In the first row behind the constables are the *matadores*, behind them the *banderilleros*, then the *picadores* and finally the mule teams used to drag out the dead bulls. When they arrive at the far side of the arena all members of the team bow to the president, the foot performers go into the alleyway, the *picadores* return to the horse yard, and the first team prepares itself.

Entry of the bull When the arena is clear the president will signal (using a white handkerchief) for the first bull to be released; trumpets sound and the door to the bull pen is opened. If you look above this door you will probably see a number; this is the weight of the bull.

What to look for A good bull will charge into the arena and attack anything which moves. It is not a good sign if a bull looks back towards the pens or is unwilling to come out, but such a bull still might perform well. Contrary to the popular Hollywood image, a bull which paws the ground before attacking is not particularly ferocious; it is in fact slightly cowardly because it is threatening without wanting to charge directly.

The first passes The *matador*, or more usually one of his assistants, will make a few passes with the large, pink-and-yellow cape to try to work out the quality of the bull. The *matador* needs to know whether it will charge, whether it can see properly, and whether it attacks better with its left or right

horn. After a few passes the president will signal for
the next act to begin.

What to look for When the *matador* takes over,
look to see if he is calm and still. Ideally he should
have his hands held low and move the cape slowly
and gracefully; he should be able to slow down the
bull's charge in this way. He should step into the
bull's path and at the moment the bull reaches him
he should be still. A step backwards is not a good
sign, so watch his feet. The proper impression that
he should give is that it is he who is in control.

The picadores The *picadores* on their horses are led
into the arena while the bull is led to a distant part.
Once the first *picador* is in position (again this usually
takes place on the shade side) the *matador* or one of
his assistants attempts to lead the bull to within a
few metres of the horse. The bull should charge, and
as it reaches the horse the *picador* should plunge the
metal-spiked tip of his lance into the large hump on
the bull's shoulders. Having received this first
wounding the bull will be led away from the horse
and lined up for a second charge.

   Officially the bull should receive three lance
thrusts, but if the *matador* judges that the bull is
losing too much strength he may ask the president
to change the act after one or two thrusts. The point
of this section of the bullfight is to reduce the
strength of the bull, but it is also to begin to break
down the strong neck muscles so that the bull charges
with its head down and thus allows the *matador* to
work closer to it.

What to look for A good bull will charge the horse
without any provocation. It will push into the horse
with its head down; if it has its head up it is trying
to reduce the pain and the effect of the lance. On
the second and third charges it will attack equally
well even though by the last charge it will probably
have associated an attack with sharp pain.

   In this act you should look to see if the *matador*
works his own bull (a good sign) or leaves it to his

assistants. As in the first act, here is the *matador*'s chance to perform beautiful passes with the large pink-and-yellow cape. You may also see the other two *matadores* making a few passes with the bull. They are allowed to do so at this point if the *matador* whose bull it is gives his permission.

A final point: many foreigners are disturbed by the fact that the horses are attacked by the bulls. Although it would be foolish to claim that this is not disconcerting or unpleasant for the horses, they are rarely injured, because they are covered in thick padding which the bull's horns cannot penetrate. They are also blindfolded on the side on which they face the bull, so they do not see it attack them.

The banderilleros   Once again the president signals for the act to be changed, the trumpets sound and the *picadores* leave the arena. For this act the *matadores* who are not performing come into the arena to help the *banderilleros* of the other *matador*. Two of the three *banderilleros* perform at this point. The first holds a *banderilla* in each hand and, once he has the bull's attention, runs in a curving path towards the bull, which is itself running towards him. When they meet he thrusts the *banderillas* into the hump on the neck of the bull and turns down its flank to escape. The second *banderillero* repeats the process and then the first places the last pair.

This act should enliven the bull after the sluggishness induced by charging the horse, and the careful placing of the *banderillas* can alter the way it charges. The *banderillas* have very small harpoon points and do not really weaken the bull; indeed they often do not actually stay in. Although it is rare, some *matadores* place their own *banderillas*, in which case this act is much more elaborate and dance-like, with music played as an accompaniment.

What to look for   Once again you should look for elegance of movement and control. At the moment of placing the *banderillas* the man should ideally have his feet together with both of them on the ground, and the *banderillas* should be placed close together in the hump. If, as he turns away from the bull, he only needs to run a few steps and is then able to walk away calmly this indicates that he is well in control and the bull is being dominated.

The final stage Once the *banderilleros* have finished their work the final act begins. With his first bull of the afternoon the *matador* will take his sword and *muleta* (the small, red, cape-like cloth), approach the presidential box, salute the president with his hat in his hand and formally ask permission to perform with and kill the bull. He may also dedicate the bull to the crowd or to an individual in the audience. If he dedicates to the crowd he will stand in the centre of the arena and salute the public with his hat, which he will then throw over his shoulder. If the hat lands brim down this is a sign of good luck; if it lands brim uppermost a sign of bad luck.

The *matador* has a whole repertoire from which to select the passes for this part of the performance, which will last about ten minutes. When he judges that it is time to kill the bull the *matador* must line it up so that its front feet are together (this makes it easier to plunge the sword in). He moves his *muleta* to get the bull to charge him and, when the two are almost in contact, leans over the horns and pushes the sword in between the shoulder blades.

Even with a good sword thrust the bull will not necessarily die immediately, but the audience will still applaud, because they are interested in seeing the man risk himself at the last moment (this is the 'moment of truth') and in the style of the sword stroke rather than in a quick death. Sometimes the *matador* is not accurate or the sword does not go completely in, in which case he must attempt to remove the sword and have another go. If the sword thrust has been effective but the bull is able to resist its death throes and is still on its feet, then the *matador* will use another sword-like instrument with which he attempts to sever the animal's spinal chord.

What to look for As with the first act you should be looking for a series of slow, graceful passes which

bring the bull under control. The *matador* should
not simply produce individual passes but rather link
one with another. He should hold the *muleta* close
to his body so that the bull almost brushes him as
it comes past. His hands should be held low and,
once again, he should step into the path of the bull
rather than step backwards. When the bullfighter
kills the bull, look to see whether he is actually
leaning over the horns and thrusting down hard so
that his hand almost touches the bull's hide.

If the bullfighter has performed badly then he will
be greeted with either silence or jeers, abuse and
whistles. If he has been reasonably good he will be
applauded and he will step into the arena to
acknowledge this. Should the applause continue, he
and his *banderilleros* will take a lap of honour. If he
has performed particularly well the crowd will wave
their white handkerchiefs (this is why you have
yours) to indicate to the president that they want an
ear of the dead bull to be awarded to the *matador*.

The awards

Officially the first ear 'belongs' to the public, and
the president should signal that it be cut if the
majority of the audience are waving handkerchiefs.
If he does not award it the whistles and jeers which
follow are for him. The public may continue waving
their handkerchiefs in petition for the second ear,
but this ear 'belongs' to the president and he does
not need to take any notice of the demands of the
public. If a *matador* is awarded an ear or ears then
he will make a lap of honour with his trophies.

Before the *matador* acknowledges any applause or
trophies the dead bull is dragged out of the arena by
a mule team. It is taken to the butchery department
where it is prepared for sale as meat. If the bull
exhibited special qualities the president may order it
to be given a lap of honour, and the audience will
stand and applaud, both for the animal itself and for
the bull breeder.

It is worth making one point about unacceptable
applause. As I said at the beginning of this chapter,
this is not the place to discuss the morality of the
bullfight and I certainly do not wish to dictate how

you should respond to it if you do attend, but there is one piece of tourist behaviour which does upset Spaniards. On various occasions I have seen *matadores* caught by bulls and badly gored, and watched foreigners stand and loudly applaud the bull. Such behaviour provoked a horrified and indignant response from Spaniards who witnessed this, for they were unable to understand how the suffering and possible death of a human being could be greeted with applause.

That, in outline, is how the performance with one bull develops, and it is a process which will be repeated six times during the afternoon. There is no procession to mark the end of the bullfight. When the last bull has been killed each *matador*, with his team of *banderilleros* behind him, crosses the arena, goes through the horse yard where the *picadores* are waiting and leaves the bullring. It is time for you to do battle with the crowd, get out of the bullring, and repair to the nearest bar to discuss the sights and impressions of the afternoon with the other *aficionados*.

Running with the bulls

The most famous events in which fighting bulls are run through the streets and those people with the nerve run with them are the San Fermin celebration in Pamplona. There are, however, other celebrations in many Spanish towns and villages where young fighting bulls are turned loose in the closed-off central square and anyone who cares to risk it may attempt to run around the animal. Bulls are not deliberately injured in these events and in Pamplona, for example, you may enter the run armed only with a rolled-up newspaper! If used correctly it can help to maintain a distance between you and an approaching animal, but a newspaper is hardly an offensive weapon against a 500-kilo bull.

Should you wish to participate it is worth bearing in mind a few fundamental points. Perhaps the most important is that although the wine drunk during the celebration may well cause you to feel that your level of courage has risen and the size of the bull somewhat diminished, the last part of the equation is only apparent – the bull does not undergo any reciprocal change. It is advisable to have a clear head in order to maintain quick reactions. Secondly, the crowd is more dangerous than the bull in the sense that they may easily block your escape, so watch to see where you can run to. Thirdly, don't run blindly. It is considerably safer if you do not, as the Spaniards say, 'lose the face of the bull'; all the time you are aware of what it is doing you have a chance to escape. The bull has four legs and a long body, so it is a lot easier for you to turn quickly than for it to do so, and a controlled escape is always possible. Finally, if you fall near the bull or otherwise get into difficulties you can be sure that someone will be there to attempt to distract the animal.

It is important to stress that there is nothing fake about these events. The bulls are real and extremely dangerous, and people, even experienced runners, are often badly injured or killed. I am not advocating that you get involved in such an event, but if you enjoy raw excitement and the thrill of adrenalin pumping through your system you will certainly find it here.

Medical matters

With luck you will not need any of the information contained in this chapter, but it is worth reading through it so that you have some idea of what facilities are available should a problem arise. Of course it is best to take out a holiday insurance policy which covers loss of luggage, money and tickets as well as medical treatment; your travel agent can advise you about the sorts of insurance available. Such medical insurance usually allows you to receive the necessary medical attention in Spain and then, with receipts from the doctor, hospital and chemists, to make a claim on your return home. Alternatively some medical insurance policies allow the doctor or hospital to make a direct claim to the company with which you are insured. It is always important to ask for a receipt for all services received, and to get a police statement if you intend to make a claim for loss or theft of luggage (see 'Emergencies').

The EEC agreement It is useful for UK nationals to note that there is an EEC agreement with regard to medical care. If you are a citizen of any EEC country you are entitled, under European Community regulations, to certain free medical treatment in Spain, but in order to receive this you must go through a complex bureaucratic procedure *before* you are even ill. It is best to be prepared with the sort of holiday medical insurance which is available through travel agents and which allows you to recoup costs incurred while abroad. If you are not a national of an EEC country then you will have to be prepared with personal medical insurance.

How the EEC scheme works If you wish to avail yourself of the medical facilities to which you are entitled in Spain, you must first obtain the *Before You Go* leaflet (SA 40) prepared by the Department of Health. This will give you basic guidance and explains whether you are entitled to free treatment abroad. Within it is an application form for the E111 form, which is the document you need to take abroad with you. The E111 should be applied for at least a month before you intend to travel. With the E111 comes a set of instructions on how to obtain free medical treatment. You must follow these procedures or you are likely to be charged private fees, and these are not refundable.

Under this scheme you are entitled to receive care on the same terms as Spanish nationals under their social security system. The difficulty is that you must take your E111 form *on arrival in Spain* to the Provincial Office *(Dirección Provincial)* of the equivalent of the DOFH, which is the *Instituto Nacional de Seguridad Social* or INSS, and the address of which you will have to find in the telephone directory. There you will be issued with a Spanish medical card and a set of vouchers which must be produced when claiming medical assistance. You are entitled to receive treatment from a doctor working within the INSS system and you will be given a list of such local doctors with the vouchers.

It is possible, if you are ill soon after arriving in Spain and have not had time to collect the vouchers, to receive free medical treatment, but only if you need treatment urgently. Details of how to make a retrospective claim are included on the explanatory notes accompanying the E111 form.

An advantage of having these documents, even if you also carry ordinary holiday insurance, is that if you decide to stay beyond the expiry date of that insurance you will have some cover; and if you are staying in Spain for an extended period, travel insurance works out to be expensive.

Getting a doctor (*un médico*)

If you are unfortunate enough to need medical treatment there are several ways of going about it. Larger hotels often have their own doctors or are in contact with various local doctors who speak English, and the reception desk will be able to arrange an appointment for you. Don't forget that if you see a private doctor you will be charged for the consultation. You should ask for a receipt and claim this from your insurance company when you return home.

If you have a minor problem which cannot be taken care of by non-prescription medicines bought at a chemist's, then you should find the nearest *ambulatorio de la seguridad social*, a national health clinic. These are open between about 09.00 and 17.00 and have an emergency service (*servicio de urgencias*) after that. Again, if you are staying in a hotel the reception desk will certainly be able to tell you where the nearest *ambulatorio* is to be found. If you are too unwell to leave the hotel then you should ask for one of the doctors to see you; this is part of their service.

For major, emergency problems you should try to get to the nearest *hospital de la seguridad social* (national health hospital). Once again, if you are in a hotel you can ask for an *ambulancia* (ambulance) to get the patient to hospital.

If you are not staying in a hotel then the address of the nearest *ambulatorio* or *hospital* can be found in the first section of the local telephone book. In that section you will also find the emergency number for calling an ambulance. Because the emergency numbers do vary from city to city it is worth remembering that the number to call for the police is 091 – if it is a *real* emergency, call them and tell them that you need an ambulance.

For problems where the patient does not need an ambulance but does need to get to a doctor quickly, it is best to go by taxi. Simply tell the driver '*Por favor, lleveme al médico o el ambulatorio/hospital más cercano*' ('Please take me to the nearest doctor or clinic/hospital'). Taxi drivers seem to enjoy dealing with such emergencies and you will quite often see a taxi, horn blaring, weaving in and out of the traffic at great speed with one of the passengers holding a white, or bloodied, handkerchief out of the window.

If the doctor you see does not speak English but you have some obvious injury, such as a cut or a broken limb, you will not need to describe symptoms. However, if it is not quite so obvious the following phrases should be useful:

Me duele la cabeza	My head hurts
el estomago	stomach
la garganta	throat
el pecho	chest
el brazo	arm
la pierna	leg
Tengo un dolor aqui. . .	I have a pain here. . . (point to the affected part)
Tengo fiebre.	I have a fever.
Me siento mareado.	I feel dizzy.
Tengo dificultad para respirar.	I have difficulty in breathing.
Estoy constipado.	I have a cold.
Me duele a barriga.	My stomach hurts.
Tengo retortijones de tripas.	I have stomach cramps.
Tengo diarrea.	I have diarrhoea.
Estoy estreñido.	I am constipated.

The doctor might well ask you '*¿Es usted alegérico a penecilina o algun otro antibiotico?*' ('Are you allergic to penicillin or any other antibiotic?') or '*¿Esta usted tomanado algunas pastillas/medicinas?*' ('Are you taking any pills/medicines?').

Dentists

Dentists (*dentistas*) rarely belong to the social security system (although they are able to extract teeth free, as part of the social security service), and so you will probably have to look for a private one. Once again, you can ask at the reception desk of your hotel for a list of local dentists, or look in the yellow pages of the telephone directory.

Chemist's (farmacia)

If the doctor prescribes any medicines, he or she will give you *una receta* (a prescription), which you will then have to take to *una farmacia* (a chemist's). *Farmacias* can be identified by the green cross which is displayed outside. They are usually open between 09.30 and 13.30 and then between 17.00 and 20.30 in the summer, and between 09.30 and 13.30 and 16.30 and 20.00 in the winter.

Even in small towns there will be a late-opening *farmacia* called a *farmacia de guardia*, and of course in cities there will be several. The *farmacia de guardia* during the day will be open continually from 09.30 to 22.00, and the night-time *farmacia de guardia* will be open from 22.00 until 09.00 the following day. There will be a notice in the window or on the door of any *farmacia* giving the address of the *farmacia de guardia* for that day. The day-time *farmacia* will be open all day for the processing of prescriptions and normal sales, but the night-time *farmacia* will *only* deal with prescriptions. There will be a red light showing outside a *farmacia de guardia* and the door will be shut, but if you ring the bell the on-call pharmacist will let you in.

After 22.00 there may be a small extra charge for prescriptions. Prescriptions for normal medicines cost about the same as in the UK. Once again, if you need medicines urgently it is best to ask a taxi driver to take you to the nearest late-opening chemist – '*Lleveme a una farmacia de guardia por favor*'.

Apart from medicines a Spanish chemist's will sell a range of non-prescribed medicines, toiletries, cosmetics and other creams and potions. If you are looking for non-prescription medicines for minor ailments such as headaches, stomach aches or diarrhoea, you can use the phrases mentioned above and the pharmacist will suggest something for your complaint. A few other useful words are:

Aspirinas	Aspirins
Paracetomol	Paracetamol
Tirita	Plaster
Venda	Bandage
Algodón	Cotton wool
Compresas higiénicas	Sanitary towels
Tampones	Tampons
Preservativas	Contraceptive sheaths
Pañales	Nappies
Papel higiénica	Toilet paper
Champú	Shampoo
Jabón	Soap
Pasta dentífrica	Toothpaste
Hojas de afeitar	Razor blades

Droguería

Although the Spanish for drugs is *drogas*, you cannot buy medicines in a *droguería*. It will sell all the non-medical items, such as toiletries, which can be purchased in a chemist's, but none of the non-prescription medicines. You will, however, be able to buy household cleaning items, paints and insecticides (*insecticidas*) and fly/mosquito sprays (*matamoscas*).

Should you be out and feel the need for an aspirin for a slight headache or bicarbonate for an upset stomach then you can ask for *aspirinas* or *bicarbonato* in a bar; something which seems particularly just, considering that such an establishment was probably the cause of the complaint in the first place.

Water and stomach complaints

Mains water is usually chlorinated and should cause you no problem, but some people do seem to suffer mild stomach upsets which might come from tap water. If you want to be safe then drink mineral water (*agua mineral*), which can be bought in grocery shops, supermarkets and bars. If you are having a meal and ask for water you should ask for either *agua mineral con gas* (carbonated mineral water) or *sin gas* (uncarbonated). Don't forget, though, if you have ice it will be made from tap water.

Emergencies

Medical emergencies, accidents, injuries and ill health are dealt with in the chapter on 'Medical matters'. Here the concern is mainly with the problems arising from being the victim of robbery or loss of personal belongings, and then the necessary encounters with the police.

Theft

Avoiding being robbed

Spanish police are concerned to advise visitors to act in such a way as to prevent unpleasant occurrences like robbery. It has already been mentioned that if you are travelling by car you should not leave anything in the car, but you should also exercise caution when on the streets. If you are staying in a hotel do make use of their safe (*caja fuerte*) and leave valuable items there. Pick-pockets and bag-snatchers tend to frequent tourist areas because of the cash, travellers' cheques and cameras which are fairly easily available.

A favourite form of bag-snatching is for two people on a motorbike to ride very close to a group of people and to snatch either a bag or a camera, which are usually loosely held, and accelerate quickly. One form of attack has even earned itself a specialist name – *un semaforazo* (literally 'a traffic lighter'). Again it features a person on a motorcycle, who approaches a potential victim who has stopped at traffic lights. The thief usually comes up on the passenger side and leans in to grab a handbag or anything else valuable. The other form of *semaforazo* is for the motorcyclist to have a brick in a bag which is used to smash a rear side window before the thief grabs things and escapes; you are therefore advised to leave nothing which can be easily removed on the back seat of the car.

Thieves can usually get away because they have the advantage of surprise and the victim is momentarily too stunned to react. A recent Spanish magazine article on the subject referred to a garage in Seville specializing in car windows which replaces on average forty broken windows a day. Tourists also often incautiously leave valuable items on tables when they are drinking outside bars; these are too easily and often snatched. Although you should not think that it is dangerous to walk the Spanish streets it is advisable to have your wallets safely tucked away and your bags securely held, to avoid tempting those few who would ruin your holiday. Police spokesmen also advise that if you do have such problems it is not worth trying to be a hero. Obviously resist if you can but, as they say, your physical well-being is worth more than the items you are likely to lose.

Of course it is not just foreigners who are robbed and even the king himself is not immune, despite his personal protectors. When shaking hands with members of the public in Seville on one occasion someone removed his Rolex, and it is also reputed that he lost a gold ring in a similar manner.

Reporting a theft

In order to make an insurance claim for the loss of property you will normally need a police report, and this can be obtained at the nearest *comisaría de la policía* (police station). In the larger cities and in many tourist areas it seems to be the policy to try to have one or two officials in the central police station who have some competence in foreign languages to help on such occasions. The form you should ask for is *la certificación de denuncia*; a form which is usually printed in both Spanish and English. You will be asked to fill this in and you will be given a copy with an official stamp. Certain words and phrases may be useful in dealing with the police on such occasions:

Quiero denunciar un robo.	I want to report a theft.
Me han robado mi. . .	My. . . has been stolen.
Bolso	Handbag
Cartera	Wallet
Maleta	Suitcase

Mochilla	Rucksack
Equipo fotográfico	Photographic equipment
Pasaporte	Passport
Divisas	Currency
Cheques de viaje	Travellers' cheques
Tarjetas de credito	Credit cards
Billetes de avion/tren	Airline/train tickets
Ropa	Clothes

Remedying the loss   Having reported your loss to the police you should immediately ring to cancel your credit cards (each company has a 24-hour telephone number for this) and your travellers' cheques (again, each company will give you instructions when you buy the cheques about exactly what to do about loss and how to have new ones issued). The loss of airline tickets will have to be sorted out with the company involved, and you must expect it to take a little longer if the tickets are with a charter company, because you will not be able to deal with this through a travel agent as you can with major national airlines. If you have lost your passport and have real financial difficulties you should contact the nearest consulate and seek help.

Consular assistance   You can find the address of the local consul by looking in the telephone directory or by asking at your hotel. Alternatively you can ring the embassy in Madrid (see 'Consular offices in Spain') and ask for the information. Most consulates have an answer-phone service giving information of office hours and an out-of-hours telephone number for emergencies.

It is worth stating fully here exactly what help a British consul can and cannot give you. (Citizens of other countries should find out before they go what help their own consul can give.) The following list is from information prepared by the Foreign and Commonwealth Office in London.

The consul *can*:

issue emergency passports (it is useful to have spare passport photographs with you).

contact relatives and friends to ask them to help you with money and tickets.

advise on how to transfer funds.

usually advance money against a sterling cheque backed by a cheque card.

as an absolute last resort, advance a loan to allow you to return home.

But a consul *cannot*:

pay for your hotel and other bills.

undertake work more properly done by travel representatives, airlines, banks or motoring organizations.

There are three main divisions of police in Spain. These are the *policía municipal* (municipal or local police), who wear blue uniforms and are mainly concerned with traffic issues, the *policía nacional* (national police), who wear lighter blue uniforms and are concerned with all matters of crime, and the *guardia civil* (civil guard), a paramilitary force who wear green uniforms and the distinctive black tricorn hat, and who are concerned with policing in rural areas and the protection of important government and official buildings. If you need to report something to the police or need their help you can of course approach any of these, but if possible it is best to find a member of the *policía nacional*. The *comisarias de policía* are staffed by members of this force.

The police

Of course it is to be hoped that you will have no such problems, but should you do so the best advice is to remain calm and be as polite and helpful as possible. Perhaps the most serious encounter you might experience is a fine (*una multa*) for speeding or overtaking. If this happens the police will fill in a short official form and fine you on the spot.

As mentioned in the 'Driving' chapter, you must have your passport and driving documents with you. All Spaniards must carry their personal identity cards with them at all times, and if you are stopped for any reason by the police they will expect you to be carrying some form of personal identification; usually a passport. Although you may well be excused if you are not carrying it, as long as there is no serious problem being investigated, it is illegal to be without

Emergencies involving the police

such a document and it can be a real nuisance if the police insist on your producing it. If you are charged with any more serious offence you should insist that the nearest consul be informed, and you will be visited as soon as possible by an official. You should also get in contact with a consul in the case of a fatal accident or any other death while abroad.

Once again it is worth listing what a consul *can* do in such serious circumstances:

provide a list of local lawyers and interpreters.
arrange for the next of kin to be informed of an accident or death, and advisde on procedures.
contact nationals who are arrested or in prison and, in certain circumstances, arrange for messages to be sent to relatives or friends.

What a consul *cannot* do is:
give legal advice, instigate court proceedings, or interfere in local judicial procedures to get you out of prison.
investigate any crime.

Emergency numbers

If you need the police, ambulance or fire brigade, try to engage the help of a nearby Spaniard. Should you have cause to have to telephone for help yourself, it is best to call the national police emergency number, which is 091, or, if you are in a rural area, the civil guard (91-411 61 62). The problem is that the person answering is unlikely to speak anything other than Spanish, so it is best to have one or two phrases prepared. You do not need complicated sentences, just a few key words such as: '*Socorro! Necesito un policía/una ambulancia/los bomberos urgentemente a . . .* ' ('Help! I need a policeman/an ambulance/the fire brigade urgently at . . .' You will then need to tell them where you are; for example in a particular street (*calle*) in a town, or if you are on the road out of town '*en la carretera . . . cerca de . . .*' ('on the . . . road . . . near'). You can also call the fire brigade by dialling 080.

Consular offices in Spain

Consular Section
British Embassy
Fernando el Santo 16
28010 Madrid
Tel: 91–419 02 00

British Vice-Consulate
Avenida de las Fuerzas Armadas 11–1
11202 Algeciras
Tel: 956–66 16 00 or 66 16 04

British Consulate
Plaza Calvo Sotelo 1/2
03001 Alicante
Tel: 965–21 67 90 or 21 61 90

British Consulate-General
Edificio Torre de Barcelona
Avenida Diagonal 477–13
08036 Barcelona
Tel: 93–322 21 51

Hon. British Vice-Consulate
Edificio Paris 1A
Calle Ruzafa
03500 Benidorm
Tel: 965–85 01 23

British Consulate-General
Alameda de Urquijo 2–8
48008 Bilbao
Tel: 94–415 76 00 or 415 77 11

British Vice-Consulate
Avenida de Isidoro Macabich 45
07800 Ibiza
Tel: 971–30 18 18 or 30 38 16

British Consulate
Edificio Cataluña
Luis Morote 6
35007 Las Palmas
Tel: 928–26 25 08

British Consulate
Edificio Duquesa
Duquesa de Parcent 8–1
29001 Malaga
Tel: 952–21 75 71 or 21 23 25

British Consulate
Plaza Mayor 3D
078002 Palma de Mallorca
Tel: 971–71 24 45 or 71 60 48

Hon. Vice-Consul
Torret 28
San Luis
07710 Menorca
Tel: 971–36 64 39

British Vice-Consulate
Plaza Weyler 8–1
38003 Santa Cruz de Tenerife
Tel: 922–28 68 63

Hon. British Consulate
Plaza de Pereda 27
39004 Santander
Tel: 9942–22 00 00

British Consulate
Plaza Nueva 8
91001 Seville
Tel: 954–22 88 75

Hon. British Consulate
Calle Real 33, 1–1
43004 Tarragona
Tel: 977–22 08 12

British Consulate
Plaza de Compostela 23–6
36201 Vigo
Tel: 986–43 71 33

American Embassy   **American**
Calle Serrano 75
Madrid
Tel: 91–276 3400/3600

American Consulate
Via Layetana 33
Barcelona
Tel: 93–319 9550

American Consulate
Avenida de Ejercito 11–3
Bilbao
Tel: 940–1435 8300

American Consulate
Paseo de las Delicias 7
Sevilla
Tel: 954–23 18 84/85

Canadian Embassy   **Canadian**
Nuñez de Balboa 35
Madrid 28001
Tel: 431–4300

Australian Embassy   **Australian**
Paseo de la Castellana 143
Madrid 28046
Tel: 279–85004/3/2/1

There is no New Zealand Embassy in Madrid. The   **New Zealand**
usual advice is that New Zealand nationals who need
consular services should go to the British or Australian
embassy.

Language and culture courses

There is an enormous range of opportunities for those who wish to go to Spain in order to learn the language and something of the culture in the formal setting of a school. Many of the universities offer courses (ranging from beginner to advanced level) for foreigners, and there are dozens of private language schools offering a variety of courses. It is impossible to list these here, but if you are interested you can obtain lists of addresses from the Spanish Institute in London. The list of language and culture courses gives information about the prices and the sort of accommodation available, but what the Spanish Institute will not do is recommend or evaluate particular courses.

Enquiries should be addressed to:

The Spanish Institute
102 Eaton Square
London SW1W 9AN
UK

The Spanish Institute
684 Park Avenue
New York
NY 10022
USA

Index